AGAINST ODDS

BY BASIL HEATTER

The Black Coast:
The Story of the PT Boat

The Sea Dreamers

Eighty Days to Hong Kong:
The Story of the Clipper Ship

"Wreck Ashore!"

Against Odds

AGAINST ODDS

BASIL HEATTER

FARRAR, STRAUS & GIROUX
NEW YORK

AN ARIEL BOOK

Contents

AGAINST ODDS

Foreword

This is a book about courage. Courage is not so easy to define. It is many things to many people: a soldier charging an enemy machine-gun nest; a boy walking through a graveyard at night and keeping his feet from running away with him; a lone sailor setting out in a small boat to cross the ocean; a blind man crossing a crowded street. It is a fireman going into a burning house. It is a matador entering the bullring. And it is any child's first day in a new school.

A famous writer who had thought a lot about courage once said that it was "grace under pressure." In this book you will meet people who have displayed more than simple grace under pressure. They have shown what it truly means to be a man or a woman—to have within you a strange, secret, tough, rubbery, indestructible bit of fiber that can be bent, twisted, stretched, whipped or torn, but never totally destroyed. It is within all of us, and it is because of that secret root of toughness and courage that we are able to cross oceans or fly to the moon or climb mountains to the top of the world, for all of us, each day of our lives, are working against odds.

I   *Point of No Return*

He was a big man in a small plane, sitting with his knees scrunched up under his chin. He would have to sit that way for a very long time and the discomfort would add to the strain. The windshield was so small he could barely see out of it, but there would not be much to see. He had no parachute. A chute would have added another twenty pounds of dead weight, and, in any case, it would not have done him any good in the sea.

He was a young man with a baby face, an obscure mail pilot. His name was Charles A. Lindbergh and he was about to attempt the most hazardous flight in the history of aviation.

The plane was called the *Spirit of St. Louis.* It was a small silver plane that can be seen today suspended from the ceiling of the Smithsonian Institution in Washington, D.C. By today's standards, it looks hardly bigger than a toy. Yet in 1927, when Lindbergh flew it nonstop from New York to Paris, it was a marvel.

The idea of flying the Atlantic did not originate with Lindbergh. Four men had already been killed in the attempt and two others were missing. The problem was to carry enough gas and still to be able to get a big, overloaded, three-engine plane off the ground. Lindbergh thought he had the answer to that—go alone in a small plane with a single engine.

Suicide, said most of the people he talked to. Insane, said the others. What happens if your engine fails? Lindbergh shrugged. He had been flying single-engine planes on the mail run at night over mountains and through storms. If his engine failed, he would have hardly a better chance in the mountains than he would have in the sea.

But his was a voice in the wilderness. No one took him as seriously as he took himself. Admiral Richard E. Byrd, the polar explorer, was about to attempt a transatlantic flight, as were Clarence Chamberlin and the French war ace, René Fonck. These were the men who occupied the headlines. There was not much room left for the gangling, boyish mail pilot from Little Falls, Minnesota.

6

All the same, Lindbergh went ahead with his plans. First he had to find a suitable aircraft. He had been flying the twin-winged biplane, basically the same plane that had been developed in World War I. It was all right for the mail route, but it hadn't the range necessary for a transatlantic flight. What was needed was a fast single-wing plane with enormous fuel capacity. Such a plane had recently been developed by a designer named Bellanca, but the manufacturers would not sell it to Lindbergh. They would not risk their reputation on so mad a stunt with an unknown pilot.

So Lindbergh had to look elsewhere. At last he found a small manufacturer in California who would build him the plane he required. He flew to California for a series of conferences with the designer and returned when the plane was ready. The first time he saw it—a small, silver monoplane gleaming in the sun—he thought it the most beautiful thing he had ever beheld. He named it the *Spirit of St. Louis,* for the people of that city had put up the money to build it.

The plane was everything Lindbergh could have hoped for, and now the dream was becoming reality. Never before had a plane been designed so expressly for a single purpose and around a single man. The allowance for the pilot was exactly Lindbergh's own weight —170 pounds—and a place had been hollowed out over his head to allow for his six-foot three-inch height.

The question of weight was uppermost in Lindbergh's

7

mind. Every pound saved meant a few extra ounces of gasoline. It became such an obsession with him that he even did without gauges on the gas tanks. He would figure his fuel consumption by the engine revolutions and his grandfather's old nickel-plated watch. A stamp collector offered to pay him a thousand dollars—half of the total amount of money Lindbergh had in the world —if he would carry a pound of airmail to Paris. But with the cold logic that guided all his actions, he refused. If he crashed in the sea, the thousand dollars would do him no good; conceivably, that one extra pound could make a difference to the success of the flight.

He took no radio because a radio was heavy and without it he could carry an extra ninety pounds of gasoline. He ripped spare pages out of his notebook and even discarded the sections of charts which covered the areas over which he did not expect to fly. He had special flight boots designed with soles a few ounces lighter than normal. His personal supplies consisted only of five sandwiches and a quart of water. He would make it on that or not at all.

On both sides of the ocean, fever was beginning to mount. Lindbergh's competitors had already gathered in New York with their various planes but were meeting with all sorts of difficulties. As Lindbergh had suspected, the planes were too big and too difficult to get off the ground. Meanwhile, in Paris, three more planes were being readied for a flight to New York. To add spice to the occasion, a prize of $25,000 had been offered to the first man to make the nonstop transatlantic flight.

On his flight from California to New York, Lindbergh had set a new transcontinental speed record. Now the previously unknown pilot found himself a celebrity, and reporters dogged his footsteps. Two things had been established: first, the *Spirit of St. Louis* was a marvelous little plane; and second, Lindbergh was the man who could fly her. His projected flight across the ocean was no longer considered a joke or a stunt. Now his every move was watched by the press and the public. Because of all this attention, Lindbergh was finding it increasingly difficult to take care of the numerous things he had to do. He lived in an atmosphere of cameras, flashbulbs, and questions. Even on the night before his takeoff, when he needed every minute of rest he could get, reporters would not leave him alone. This shy young Middle Westerner, who would shortly find himself one of the most famous men in the world, already hated publicity with a passion. In his modesty he carried letters of introduction to people in Europe, as if the first man to fly the Atlantic would need an introduction.

At last Lindbergh's preparations were complete. The plane was as ready as it would ever be. On May 19 he went to bed still undecided: would he or would he not attempt to lift the heavily overloaded *Spirit of St. Louis* off the ground at dawn? Standing at his hotel window, too

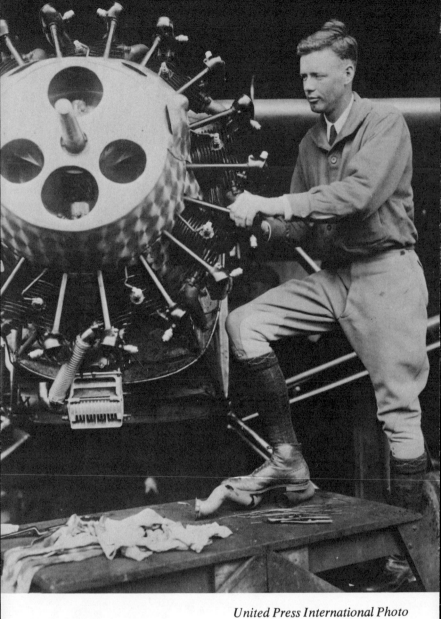

Charles Lindbergh inspects the engine of *The Spirit of Saint Louis.*

restless to sleep, he could see a drizzling mist hanging over the city. The weather was not promising. Outside his door, the reporters were clamoring for interviews. He finally dressed and went downstairs at 3 a.m. The fog and rain thickened as he drove out to the airport.

Still undecided, he ordered the plane wheeled out of the hangar. The mechanics watched; the crowds outside the fence watched. Lindbergh looked up at the wind sock. The wind had shifted from east to west. That was bad. Instead of a head wind to assist him in his takeoff, he now had a tail wind. If he wanted an excuse not to go, this was certainly it. No one would have thought him lacking in courage if he had gone back to his hotel and turned in.

But Lindbergh said nothing. He climbed up into the cockpit and pulled the goggles down over his eyes. Still he had not decided. "It was the kind of feeling," he said later, "that comes when you gauge the distance to be jumped between two stones across a brook." Finally, sitting there in the cockpit, he knew he would make the jump. It was a decision resulting not so much from logic as from feeling. The feeling was right and he had to trust it.

The plane lurched down the runway, agonizingly slow on the muddy ground. The thousands of people who had assembled even at that hour seemed to hold their breath. Were they about to see the start of a historic flight or the fiery death of a brash young fool? Once he had started, there would be no turning back. The overloaded plane

11

would either leave the ground in time or crash through the fence at the end of the field.

Now the spot of silver, caught like a bug in the glare of the searchlights, was moving faster. The wheels left the ground and then the plane bounced down again. The crowd groaned. But now she was up once more. Higher this time. Air space between the wheels and the ground. Higher still. The motor whined as Lindbergh gunned it to the maximum. He had cleared the fence. There were electric cables ahead; he cleared them by less than twenty feet. The crowd let out a roar of appreciation as the plane headed out into the watery dawn.

Two hours later Lindbergh was approaching the coast of Nova Scotia, his first navigational checkpoint. Here the plane would begin to handle more easily, since, with each passing hour, he was using more and more of the immense overload of fuel. Already the plane was four hundred pounds lighter than when he had started.

So far, all was well. The engine ran beautifully and his navigation was practically on the nose (only about six miles off course). But there was a new danger—a deadly sleepiness. The persistence of the newspaper reporters the night before, and his own restlessness, had made it impossible for him to sleep before taking off, and now he had been awake twenty-four hours. Time and again Lindbergh's eyes closed and his chin sagged forward onto his chest. He would awake with a start and a sensation of terrible danger, only to find the same thing happening a few minutes later. He felt panic welling up. If

12

he couldn't stay awake, what chance would he have? And the flight was just beginning; he had more than thirty hours to go.

Three hours later he was over the tip of Nova Scotia and heading toward Newfoundland across two hundred miles of water. The worst was still to come—the worst in terms of exhaustion and of total commitment. Even then, Lindbergh might still have turned back. A pilot likes to enjoy his options—that is, the ability to meet a possible emergency with a variety of choices. One by one, Lindbergh was running through his options. When he reached the point of no return—when he had used up half his fuel—he would have no more options and there would then be no choice but to go straight ahead.

Lindbergh was flying into night, a lonely two thousand miles of black night and heaving ocean. He was as alone as it is possible on this earth for a man to be. If his motor faltered, if his wings iced, he would go down into that black sea and no one would have the faintest idea where he was. Without a radio, he could not get off the feeblest sort of cry for help.

The terrible need for sleep continued to threaten him, so urgent now that for the first time he thought he would not be able to complete the flight after all. Sleep would murder him, creep up on him unawares and send him plunging into the sea.

He actually pried his eyes open with his fingers, but the lids crept down anyway. Certainly he must have dozed briefly for a few seconds at a time without knowing it.

13

Yet his trained pilot's nerves and reactions were always there to save him if the ship registered a change in altitude or air speed. Despite his exhaustion, Lindbergh's mind was like some marvelous computerized instrument, sensitive to the slightest variation.

At the end of eighteen hours he knew that he was approximately halfway to Paris—but that was all. He would not really know where he was until he sighted land, and even then it might be the wrong land.

As the sun rose, Lindbergh found himself slowly winning the battle against sleep. He was in the grip of a curious phenomenon known to singlehanded sailors and solitary pilots: if you drive the body hard enough, you experience the same sort of second wind achieved by a runner who seems to have reached his last gasp. The stupor that had held Lindbergh for hours was beginning to fade. He found himself more alert, better able to make his log entries and adjust his fuel mixture. He was like an invalid getting over a long illness. His eyes stayed open without effort now, and his sense of feel and smell returned. He was even able to munch at a sandwich for the first time since the flight had begun.

In the twenty-sixth hour of his flight, he saw his first sea bird and had the comforting feeling that he might be approaching land. Though he did not know how far offshore any birds might be found, he did not suppose it could be more than a few hundred miles.

A short time later he saw a fishing trawler at work

below him and felt a sudden charge of excitement. He circled low over the trawler, shouting through his open window, "Which way to Ireland?" but was unable to get an answer. Possibly the amazed fisherman was speechless at seeing a plane approach from the west.

Lindbergh carried on and an hour later saw land ahead. But what land was it? All through the hours of darkness it had been impossible to estimate exactly his drift or speed made good, so he didn't know if what he saw ahead was Ireland, Scotland, or even the coast of Europe itself. As the plane drew closer, there was no mistaking the high mountains and emerald-green valleys of Ireland. Lindbergh was on course—amazingly close in fact, only three miles from the point at which he had hoped to arrive. Altogether, it was an astonishingly accurate landfall. He was flooded by a sense of relief. He was now only four hours from Paris, the engine was running smoothly, and he still had plenty of gas left. For the first time he allowed himself to believe that the worst was over and that he was actually going to make it.

It was still daylight when he arrived over the coast of France, an hour from Paris. No longer tired, he felt that he could have gone on even farther, but he had already passed the 3,500-mile mark and had set a new world's record for nonstop flight. Paris would do well enough. To celebrate, he ate a sandwich and was about to toss the wrapper out of the open window when he thought better of it. He didn't want his first contact with Europe

15

to be a discarded bit of wastepaper. It is somehow typical of the man that such a thought should have entered his head at that time.

It was dark when Lindbergh came in over Paris and followed the blaze of light toward the airfield. From above he could see one of the greatest traffic jams in history as hundreds of thousands of people and cars struggled toward the airport. With his usual modesty he put it down to the late-evening traffic jam, not realizing that all of Paris was rushing to the airport to greet him.

At 10:22 Paris time, his wheels touched the ground. The crowd, which had been held back by the fixed bayonets of a regiment of soldiers, broke through the barricade and dashed across the field toward him. He was afraid that his spinning propeller might injure someone, but he had landed exactly in the center of the huge field and by the time they reached him the engine had stopped. Hands extended to drag him from the plane. His leather helmet was torn from his head. His carefully kept logbook was snatched away and never returned. For a moment or two he was actually in the greatest danger of his trip—of being crushed to death by the madly cheering crowd. Fortunately, a quick-witted officer pointed to a tall man on the outskirts of the crowd and shouted, "There goes Lindbergh!" In the confusion that followed, Lindbergh himself slipped away.

He was at that moment certainly the most famous flyer in history and perhaps the most famous man in the world. You might wonder what his first words were as

16

the plane stopped and the door opened and the hands reached out to him. Lindbergh said, "Does anybody here speak English?"

A thoroughly practical question.

2   *On Top of the World*

They stood where no men had ever been before, at 360
degrees of longitude—literally on top of the world—
with one foot in the Eastern Hemisphere and the other in
the West. The date was April 6, 1909. After years of
struggle they were at the North Pole. From that tremendous moment, one was to go on to become a United
States Navy admiral, the other to a job parking cars.
Their names were Robert Peary and Matthew Henson.
One was white, the other black.

They had met in a hat store in Washington, D.C.,
where Lieutenant Peary, assigned to an engineering sur-
vey of the Panama Canal, had gone to buy a pith helmet
as protection against the tropical sun. The hats were car-

ried in from the storeroom by a slender young black clerk named Henson. Peary was searching for someone to look after his things on the expedition. Within five minutes, young Matt had agreed to go along.

Matt Henson was an unusual boy in many ways. This was not the first time he had ventured to one of the earth's far places. He had spent five years as a sailor on a square-rigger and knew his way from Hong Kong to Cape Horn. But in 1885 there were few opportunities for black men, no matter how energetic and ambitious, and he had wound up as a stock boy in the hat store in Washington. The chance to go off with Peary, even in the lowly position of body servant, was too good to miss.

But the trip to the jungles was only the beginning. Peary's real dream lay in the white wastes of Greenland. For three centuries expeditions of various kinds had been attempting to reach the North Pole and all had failed, almost always with a heavy loss of life. Now the young American lieutenant believed that he could be the one to succeed. He had conceived a plan of staggering audacity —to cross the northern tip of Greenland by dog sled and then venture far out on the icecap to the very top of the world, where no man had ever been before. To most men it would have remained a dream, but Peary, a coldly efficient engineer and superb organizer, had a way of converting dreams into reality. As a schoolboy he had written his mother, "Today as I think of what the world is and that I have my life before me, nothing seems impossible." Not even the North Pole, as it turned out.

The lure of the North was like a fever in Peary's blood. Even during the steamiest days in the jungles of Nicaragua he thought about it and talked about it, and after three months of association with Matt Henson it was pretty well decided between them that if Peary ever did succeed in organizing a polar expedition young Matt would go along.

But first, and perhaps even more disheartening than the search for the Pole itself, came the task of raising money for the expedition. Peary was wise enough not to say right off the bat that he was making an attempt on the Pole. On the last expedition in search of the Pole, seventeen men had starved to death, and the time before that, only two men had survived. Who then would put up the money for a brash young lieutenant to attempt what was obviously an impossibility? Realizing that, Peary announced a less ambitious plan, although still dangerous and daring enough. He would travel by sled across Greenland near the 80th parallel in an attempt to reach the northeast coast, where no man had ever been. Sums of money from various scientific and geographic organizations began to reach Peary, but there was never really enough. When he had added up the expense of chartering a ship and transporting the expedition to Greenland, he found he had just eight dollars left, hardly enough to pay a salary to any of his assistants. When he told Henson that if he wanted to join the expedition he would have to go as an unpaid volunteer, young Matt just smiled, nodded, slid the hatboxes back on the

20

shelf, and marched out of the store without so much as a backward look.

Peary reckoned that the distance to the coast and back was twelve hundred miles, a journey of two and a half months. The greatest problem would be to carry enough food. With luck, they might kill an occasional seal or musk ox, but they could not count on it. Their basic food would be pemmican—dried beef mixed with fat, sugar, and raisins. In addition they would have tea, condensed milk, hardtack, and dehydrated soup. The best months for traveling on the icecap would be May, June, and July, when there would be twenty-four hours of daylight and the sun would not yet have softened the snow.

First they would have to build some sort of semi-permanent winter quarters on the ice, from which the party could make its dash in the spring. At that work Henson proved invaluable, for he had a natural flair for carpentry and prefabricated all the parts of the houses while the party was still on board ship. The second step would be the recruiting of Eskimos; there again, Henson was invaluable. While the Eskimos at the top of the world kept aloof from white men, they believed Matt's brown skin made him one of their own and immediately responded by calling him Innuit, the name Eskimos call themselves. Later, as they learned to love him for his kindness and to respect him for his wisdom, they called him Marri Palook, "dear little Matthew." The confidence of the Eskimos in Matt Henson was to be one of the greatest assets of the expedition.

Matthew Henson. The photograph is from the collection of Admiral Robert Peary, © National Geographic Society, courtesy Robert E. Peary, Jr., and Mrs. Marie Peary Kuhne.

A winter on the ice was a cruel business, but the party survived it and crossed Greenland as planned. Peary returned to New York a hero. He was not content, for in his heart he knew that all this was only preliminary to the real effort—a dash for the Pole. But this aim was not to be discussed openly, for there were too many other explorers ready to beat him to the punch if possible. The Norwegian government had already agreed to finance the expedition of Fridtjof Nansen to the Pole. Peary, still forced to raise funds by private subscription, knew that time was against him. He resolved to return the following spring to Greenland and the icecap and already had Henson's promise to go with him.

They did return the next spring and again the following year. Each time they came closer to the Pole but each time were driven back by great storms or depleted supplies. Once they were within a week of it—just one more week to the Pole—but they couldn't make it. They had gone thirty miles closer than any previous expedition, but the dogs were dying of starvation and the men were haggard ghosts stumbling blindly through the snow in their bulky furs. They might reach the Pole, but if they did they would never get back. It was a grim moment when Peary decided to turn back. Matt Henson, who had followed him through one ordeal after another, felt the tears ooze from his eyes and freeze on his cheeks. To have come so close, closer than any other men, and then be forced to turn back for at least another year or perhaps forever was a heartbreaking thing for both of

23

them. But when Peary raised his arm and pointed back the way they had come, Henson said nothing.

In 1907, when Peary was past fifty and the boyish Henson more than forty, they began to prepare for the last and greatest effort. Both were aware that if they did not make it this time they would never have another opportunity. Even if funds could be found for another expedition, they would be too old for the physical ordeal.

Once more the numerous pieces of equipment were accumulated and once more a ship to carry them north was obtained. But they were old hands now, veterans, operating with the professional ease that comes from long experience. The icy shores of Greenland would seem like a second home to them. The Eskimos they would find there would be old friends with whom they had sledged fifteen years before on earlier expeditions. When the *Roosevelt,* their ship, sailed north in July of 1908, there was not much excitement. The men were grim, almost sad. They had gathered the last of their strength for the greatest effort of all, and the knowledge that it was the final one left them with a feeling of emptiness.

Once more, houses were built and they prepared for another winter on the ice. The blackness of the polar night descended. For more than six months their world would be reduced to the flickering glow of a lantern. Through the long night they busied themselves building sleds and regrouping supplies and navigational equipment.

24

At last the sun returned. Amid the cracking of whips and the excited barking of the huskies, the sleds started north. All went well enough until they came to an opening in the ice, a stretch of water they could not cross. They settled down to camp beside the open lead until it closed, and as they waited, the Eskimos grew more and more restless. They were afraid to go farther, afraid of the evil and unknown spirits that lurked beyond the northern horizon. Peary promised them gifts of every kind if they would continue, but they shook their heads; they were determined to go home.

In despair, Peary asked Henson to speak to them. Now the Eskimos listened more attentively, their faces still expressionless but their eyes displaying a greater interest, for this was their beloved brother and friend of years past, Marri Palook, "dear little Matthew." Peary was a respected leader, but he was still a white man, whereas Henson was one of their own. At last they agreed that where Marri Palook would go they would follow. The crisis that could have destroyed the expedition at the last stage was over, and as the ice closed, they were able to move forward.

They were now only 135 miles from the Pole and still had plenty of food. The Pole was almost within their grasp when the lead sled carrying the navigational equipment broke through thin ice and began to sink. Without their sextants and chronometers, the explorers could never prove they had been to the Pole, even if they did reach it. With a desperate effort, Henson went after the

25

sled and managed to keep it from sinking farther, until the others got there to help him.

On April 5, Peary took a latitude sight and found they were only thirty-five miles from the Pole. They camped for the night, their last camp before the final dash. At midnight they started out again, and a noon sight showed them to be, at last, on top of the world.

The two old friends who had gone through so much together to achieve this moment looked into each other's eyes and gripped each other's mittened hands but could think of nothing to say. What words could possibly have expressed their feelings?

Peary and Henson returned to a world-wide reception, but strangely enough the relationship between the two men had soured. It was as if Peary, jealously guarding his fame, refused to let Matt Henson enjoy his own position as co-discoverer of the North Pole. From the day they returned, Peary never spoke to his companion again until, eleven years later, when Peary lay dying, he asked to see Henson. Marri Palook rushed to Peary's side. No one knows what the two old men said to each other in that final moment.

After that, Matt Henson was forgotten. The white organizations that had honored Peary's accomplishment neglected Henson. For thirteen years he lived in almost complete obscurity, scraping a precarious living as a parking-lot attendant. At last, in 1929, a bill was introduced into Congress demanding some federal recognition for Henson, and he was finally given a job as a *messen-*

ger boy in the Customs House. Quite a recognition from his grateful country to the co-discoverer of the North Pole!

But Matt Henson was never bitter. When asked if he didn't feel cheated, he replied that heaven had a way of evening out old scores and that he would take his chances there. In 1955, at the age of eighty-nine, Marri Palook, who had stood on top of the world, went on his final voyage of discovery.

3   *Annapurna*

---

1. The Ascent

Two men crawled slowly up an ice ridge. Ahead lay the
blazing blue sky and emptiness. Behind lay four miles of
snow, ice, and rock. They were higher than any climbers
had ever gone before.

The mountain was Annapurna and the place was
Nepal in the Himalayas, the top of the world. The year
was 1950. The men were Maurice Herzog and Louis
Lachenal. For more than two months they had been
moving with their party of climbers and porters through

the jungles of the lowlands and up the icy slopes toward the peak of Annapurna. Now, at last, Herzog and Lachenal were making the final assault. Victory lay only a few hundred yards ahead. Death was even closer.

Young and strong as they were, they moved slowly, painfully, inch by inch, like men a hundred years old. Herzog, in the lead, hardly ever looked up and never back. The pain and weariness he felt were hidden behind the large snow goggles that covered most of his face. His breath came in great shuddering gasps, but the thin air that filled his lungs had hardly enough oxygen to sustain life. Each step required an immense effort of will, a marshaling of the last dregs of energy.

Lachenal, a step or two behind, was in even worse condition. Once, as he paused for breath, he gasped into Herzog's ear, "What will you do if I cannot go on?"

"I will go alone," Herzog whispered back.

The sky, in that thin air, was burning brighter than ever. Neither of them had ever seen such a sky before. Although the slope was bathed in sunlight, the cold was so intense that both men had long since lost any sensation in their feet. Once Lachenal paused, laboriously unlaced his left boot, and rubbed the toes in an effort to restore circulation. Both had known climbers who had lost their toes after frostbite and had been crippled for life. Lachenal lived in terror of frostbite, but he fought back his fear and went on.

Step by step, they mounted higher. Both men now began to experience a sensation of happiness. The brutal

29

reality of the mountain seemed to waver and become dreamlike. The climbers were united in the brotherhood of a prodigious effort, and despite the danger, they would not have traded places with any other two men in the world.

The sky was changing, becoming a deep sapphire blue as the day advanced. The wind was now so fierce as to make it almost impossible to stand. Drifting snow hurled toward them by the wind bit into their exposed cheeks like slivers of glass.

After each step they rested on their ice axes, gasping for breath. Their hearts were thumping in such a way that it seemed they would literally burst from the chests that enclosed them. Yet Herzog and Lachenal had never been happier. For years they had been working toward this goal, training for it, directing all their energies toward it, and now at last it lay within their grasp.

Up! Up! One step more. Two steps more. Force the frozen foot to move, the frozen arm to extend the ice ax, the frozen lips and nostrils to suck in the air. One more step. One more—until at last, as Herzog gazes upward, he sees only the jewel-like blue of the sky. There is no more rock or snow or ice. There is no place to go but down. They have done it. They have reached the top. For the first time in history, men stand higher than 8,000 meters, more than four miles high in the sky. Above them there is nothing. Below, hidden by clouds, lies the world.

Lachenal seemed unimpressed. There was only one

thing on his mind—that they must get off this devilish
mountain as soon as possible. The day was dying. Their
limbs were freezing. Every minute counted. He tugged at
Herzog's arm and pointed downward.

But Herzog, who had journeyed for a lifetime toward
this moment, was not to be hurried. He fumbled in his
pack and took out his camera and a little French flag.
With hands that were now no more than frozen claws, he
tied the flag to his ice ax and took Lachenal's picture and
then held the ax aloft while Lachenal took his.

Herzog, affected by the dreamy unreality of the moment, felt as if he could stay on the mountain peak forever, but Lachenal, quite rightly, kept pointing downward and indicating that they had not a second to lose.
Even as they had stood there on the summit, the weather
had been changing. The brilliant blue sky was gone.
Clouds now obscured the peak and the wind had bite
enough in it almost to freeze the blood in their veins.
Herzog knew that Lachenal was right. If they were to
have any chance at all of coming down alive, they must
leave at once. As a final gesture, he stuck his ice ax into
the snow and left it there, the little flag whipping in the
wind. Then he turned his eyes and his steps downward.

Lachenal was already far below. Herzog turned for
one last look at the peak that had given him such joy
and at the same time so much suffering. He took out his
pocket aneroid for a reading. At that moment, although
he was hardly aware of it, his gloves slipped away. He
reached for them but they had already started down the

slope. Herzog made a desperate lunge; the gloves were gone. With horror he watched them sliding down into the abyss. Only a mountaineer who has seen the full effects of frostbite could know the anguish that filled his soul. Without his mittens he was at the very least a cripple, more likely a dead man. His only hope was to get down to camp as quickly as possible.

Lachenal, racing against time and stumbling along on frozen feet, was still far ahead. Herzog went after him. In his anxiety, he had forgotten the spare pair of socks he carried in his pocket, which could easily have substituted for the lost mittens. The mist had thickened and the howling of the wind was like that of a ravenous wolf pack. Lachenal had disappeared. Herzog continued to grope his way down. Once he stumbled and fell, and both his naked hands were plunged into the snow. Now he was on bare ice—the steepest part—saved only by his crampons, the spikes mountaineers attach to their boots. There, just ahead in the mist, was the tiny tent they had left that morning. And beside it was another tent! Two more climbers had come up to help them down.

2. The Descent

Herzog's frozen fingers had turned violet and white and were hard as wood. He felt no pain yet; that would come later, a pain beyond description.

Suddenly, from out of the mist far below the tents, he and the two other climbers—Terray and Rebuffat—heard a faint cry for help. It was Lachenal, who had gone on ahead and had taken a terrible fall that had left him stunned and in a state of collapse. They rushed down to help him, but Lachenal fought them. He knew that his feet were frozen and he was in deadly fear of amputation. His only thought was to get down to the base camp, where he could be treated by the doctor. Yet the only hope for any of them was to get into the flimsy shelter of the tents immediately. Despite his protests, the half-stunned Lachenal was dragged back up to the tents.

Outside, the storm howled and the snow was still falling. The mist grew thick and darkness came. The four men had to cling to the poles to prevent the tents from being blown away. It was a hellish night. Lachenal and Herzog were in great pain as Terray and Rebuffat rubbed, slapped, and beat at them with rope ends in an effort to restore circulation to the frozen limbs.

In the morning they began the descent. Herzog, his hands frozen, was helpless. They had to tie his boots for him and then fasten him like a child onto the rope as they went down through the blizzard. But the fresh snow had obscured all their landmarks. They could see hardly more than a few yards ahead and they were never sure of where they were. All four climbers were now in deadly danger. Their tents had been left behind; if they didn't reach the base camp by afternoon, they would be finished. None could have survived a night on the open

33

slopes. Lachenal was half out of his mind. Terray and Rebuffat were now beginning to suffer from frostbite. None of them had eaten since the day before.

The hours dragged by. Herzog thought he recognized the trail to the camp and pointed in that direction, but after they had followed that way a while they came up against a sheer ice wall. It was too dark to go any farther. The next day they were to find that just beyond the ice wall, only thirty yards ahead, was the camp they had been looking for.

Their only chance for survival was to find a crevasse or ravine that would shelter them from the wind. But there was nothing. They were on an exposed slope and facing certain death. Hopelessly, Terray began to dig a hole with his ice ax. Lachenal, babbling to himself, had wandered off to the side. Suddenly he let out a yell and disappeared. He had fallen through the thin coating of snow into a crevasse and was lying unhurt at the bottom. By a miraculous chance, he had fallen into a hole that was big enough for all of them. They scrambled down after him.

The cold in the grotto of ice was even worse than it had been above, but at least they were out of the wind. They huddled together without speaking. Just to open one's mouth was an expenditure of precious energy.

All night they sat there. The minutes seemed as long as hours and the hours as long as days. The only motion was the weary massaging of frozen hands or feet.

Somehow the night passed. Slowly a blue light began

to spread through their icy chamber. From outside came the tremendous roar and mutter of an avalanche. Herzog could now vaguely make out the shape of his companions' features in the dim light and he indicated it was time to go. Rebuffat and Terray objected, saying it was still pitch black. Herzog realized with a sinking heart that his two rescuers, having taken off their snow goggles the day before in an effort to find the path, were now suffering from snow blindness. They could see nothing at all. Now all four were crippled in one way or another.

In addition to everything else, they could no longer put on their boots, which they had taken off during the night to massage their frozen toes. Their feet were so swollen that it was impossible to get the boots back on. Herzog was now barefoot as well as bare-handed. His hands were so useless that he could not even climb out of the crevasse, but somehow the others pushed and pulled him upward. They had no longer any hope of survival or rescue. Yet it seemed better to die in the open than in that dank hole in the ice.

They could go no farther. The two blind men were as helpless as babies. Lachenal was raving. Herzog felt the breath leaving his body and knew that he was dying. Yet somehow they mustered the strength for one last despairing cry for help. The sound of their voices was blown away on the wind. Nothing. They sank down into the snow. And at that moment they heard an answering cry!

Barely two hundred yards away, waist deep in the snow, stood Schatz, a member of the base-camp force.

35

Behind him came others. All was not lost after all. Herzog was losing consciousness fast, but he still had enough strength left to manage a smile as Schatz reached him and threw his arms around him.

3. Agony

Their lives had been saved, but the torment was just beginning. They were still at 8,000 meters and the monsoon could close in on them again at any moment. The crippled men had to be lowered on the rope like children. Now that the sky was clear again after the storm, the blazing sun was working on the masses of fresh snow, threatening to send them booming down the mountain. Only a climber in the Himalayas can visualize the fury of an avalanche at those altitudes.

Once, as they were descending to Base Camp Two, Herzog became aware of a crack opening in the snow under his feet. He made an effort to scramble higher, but it was too late. He was picked up by a superhuman force and whirled end over end through the air. When he regained consciousness, he found himself hanging head down from the rope, dangling above the abyss. Slowly he managed to work his way toward the face of the mountain.

Once again Herzog had been incredibly lucky. He and two of the Sherpas, natives who were acting as porters, had been torn loose from the main party. The avalanche hurled them through the air and they had come to rest on opposite sides of an ice ridge, where their weight had counterbalanced each other. If the rope had not held. . . . But there had been so many ifs already that one more hardly seemed to matter.

Herzog's hands were in a ghastly condition. The flesh was laid bare and red, and the rope he had been clutching was covered with blood. Every movement of his fingers meant the loss of another strip of flesh. Moreover, the frostbite in his legs was getting worse; he could feel it now spreading right up through the calves of his legs toward his thighs. And, along with everything else, his snow goggles had been snatched away, so that he was now blinded by the intense light.

One of the Sherpas found another pair of goggles for Herzog and slipped them over his face. When he tried to restore Herzog's mittens, the sight of those torn and bleeding hands was too much and he had to turn away to be sick. But somehow, though the wounded men were barely clinging to life, they went on.

At Base Camp Two, Doctor Oudot was waiting for them. He examined Herzog first and was appalled by what he found. There was practically no skin left on his hands; the little that remained hung down in long, blackened strips. His feet had long since lost any feeling and had turned the color of dark wood. As for Lachenal, although his hands had not been affected, his feet were in not much better shape then Herzog's. Both Rebuffat and

37

Terray were completely blind, but that was a temporary condition which would begin to clear up after a few days of treatment. It seemed likely that Lachenal would lose his toes and perhaps part of the foot itself, but it was even more likely that Herzog would lose all his fingers as well as his feet. Although they were still at 20,000 feet and clinging to the side of the mountain, the doctor at once began a series of injections. As he injected the needle into Herzog's thigh, he was horrified to find that the wounded man's blood had turned quite black and was as thick as pudding.

They were still faced with the problem of getting down the rest of the way. The helpless men would have to be carried on the porters' backs. Hourly they were given intensely painful injections. Herzog found himself weeping like a child at the thought of the needle. He howled like a dog and two men had to hold him motionless while the doctor did his work.

It took them five incredible weeks to make the descent. Herzog, his hands and legs wrapped in enormous bandages, rode on a Sherpa's back. Though Herzog was almost twice the size of the man who carried him, somehow the Sherpa maintained his footing and carried his load over the ice without falling. Behind them, always present, came the doctor with his needle.

Somehow they staggered on, day after day. At last they were off the mountain and down into the jungle. Now they were subjected to intense heat and the furious monsoon rains. Clouds of insects swarmed over the

Maurice Herzog greeting members of the British Expedition who climbed Mt. Everest. Note his right hand, damaged by frostbite.

wounded men. Herzog's fingers and toes snapped off and fell away like dead sticks. The doctor performed endless operations. At last they were at Katmandu and the railway to New Delhi and finally the plane to Paris.

And so they had done it: conquered the mountain and survived. But at what a price! You may ask yourself if it was worth it. The answer to that is something each of us must provide for himself. Each man has his own Annapurna. Herzog's body was half destroyed, but his unconquerable spirit remained cleaner and stronger than before—as clean and strong as the peak of Annapurna itself, shining in the sky.

4   *Torpedoes Away!*

Out of the fog, high and ominous on the gray water, came the Japanese ships. They moved into battle line, inviting the Americans to attack. To the men on the U.S. destroyer *Bailey* it appeared an invitation to death, for they were hopelessly outgunned. But the *Bailey* had been ordered to attack and now, at 30 knots, she was flinging herself like David's stone toward the enemy Goliath.

It had been a strange day in a strange war. The year was 1943 and for the first time in almost a hundred and fifty years enemy forces had landed on American soil. The Japanese had occupied the Aleutian islands of Kiska and Attu off the coast of Alaska—a very long way from the American mainland, to be sure, but American territory all the same. Now the small American task force of cruisers and destroyers was prowling the icy seas at the top of the world, hunting for an enemy convoy.

For days the crews had seen nothing but fog and wind-whipped seas. The screeching blast of the Alaskan storm, the "williwaw," howled in the rigging and plucked with a cutting edge at the faces of the men on watch. Gingerly the gray ships made their way through heaving seas. Visibility in the sleet storms and blinding blizzards was sometimes less than zero. Only the far-seeing radar could penetrate the murk. When at last the electronic eye revealed a series of targets somewhere out in the sleet, the Americans, believing that what they saw were the waddling ships of a convoy bound for Attu, closed in for the kill.

As the fog lifted, they saw no clumsy merchant ships ahead. Instead, there were the tall turrets and menacing guns of Japanese heavy cruisers. It was too late to turn back. The exposed and outnumbered Americans had no choice but to fight. Rear Admiral C. H. McMorris, on the light cruiser *Richmond,* ordered all ships to concentrate on his flagship and to form for battle at 25 knots. One by one, in the red glow of dawn, the enemy ships hove over the horizon. Two heavy and two light cruisers were identified, along with a cluster of destroyers. The Americans were outnumbered two to one.

The Japanese held to an easterly course, cutting the American task group from its base. On board the Ameri-

42

can ships, final preparations for battle were completed. The men stood to general quarters. The majority had never been in battle before, so this struggle against great odds was a rude introduction. Few expected to survive it.

The two American cruisers, *Richmond* and *Salt Lake City,* closed up, with two destroyers, *Bailey* and *Coughlan,* off the light cruiser's port bow and the other two off the heavy cruiser's starboard quarter.

The enemy concentrated his guns on the *Salt Lake City,* the only American ship capable of trading equal fire at long range with the Japanese cruisers. Once the *Salt Lake City* was finished, they could deal with the smaller American ships. But the *Salt Lake City,* although untried in battle, was tough. She scored first blood with a hit on the Japanese flagship, the heavy cruiser *Nachi.* The two forces were still far apart, twelve miles or more, and the *Richmond* and her destroyer screen could do little but bark their encouragement like terriers yapping at the heels of mastiffs.

The American heavy cruiser's decks leaped with the enormous thunder of her guns. Sixteen times she fired full salvos, sending tons of metal screeching through the air. On the fourth salvo a blossom of flame appeared on the *Nachi*'s bridge and a great column of smoke climbed into the sky. A moment later the Japanese flagship was hit again, this time near the forward stack, and once again she gushed smoke.

But the *Salt Lake City*'s incredible luck was running out. She had been straddled by shell after shell and had

43

somehow maneuvered between them, but now she too was taking punishment. The enemy ships showed in dark silhouette against the gray horizon, illuminated by clusters of orange flame as they fired full salvos at thirty-second intervals. The range was closing, and *Salt Lake City,* firing five guns to the enemy's twenty, was in a precarious position. Time after time the splashes of a salvo seemed to walk up from astern and on past her as she knifed through the water at full speed.

Then the American heavy cruiser took her first hit. She leaped and shuddered and seemed to stand still in the water. But the blow had been a glancing one. A shell, falling steeply, had glanced off her hull near the waterline and exploded in the water only a few feet away from the ship's side. The shock had been cruel and had stopped her in her stride, but the ship's skin was unbroken and now she leaped forward again.

The Japanese flagship, hit again, had slowed her pace and *Salt Lake City* was fighting hard. Her guns, white-hot, thundered without pause. Her gun crews, intent on their duties, danced the strange dance of men in combat to the clack and hiss of breechblocks opening and the roar of compressed air shooting into the gun barrels. There were cries of "Bores clear!" and screeching whistles as men lifted and lunged and the loading trays clashed in the open breeches. Ramming levers jerked forward and back, powder bags were shoved against the shells with a heavy slither, breechblocks swung and closed with hissing, clashing impact. Then the great muz-

44

zles were elevating, seeming to sniff the sky and the enemy. The firing buzzer sounded a warning and the shell was hurled into space with a tremendous crash and concussion. Then once again the gunners, sweating despite the cold, resumed their strange wild dance.

But now the *Salt Lake City* was hit a second time. She seemed to ring all over like a giant bell, trembling with shock as an enemy shell punched through her side above the waterline. For the better part of two hours the big American ship had fought off the two heavy cruisers and had given far more than she had received. She had steamed through a hell of exploding shells, which had poured down on her by the hundreds, and had somehow evaded all but two. But her good fortune could not last. A minute later she took her third hit, and then a fourth.

Now there were dead and wounded men on board the *Salt Lake City,* and streams of water and oil burst from her insides like blood. Down below, men waist deep in water and oil fought the rising sea while above decks the guns still blazed, but it appeared to be a losing fight. If the water rose only a few more inches, it would flood the main engines and the *Salt Lake City* would be dead in the water.

Sensing that his heavy cruiser was in desperate trouble, Admiral McMorris ordered the destroyers in to lay smoke around her as a protective measure. The little ships leaped forward around the stricken ship while shells burst around them and black smoke poured from their funnels. Behind the smoke the wounded *Salt Lake*

45

City lay breathing heavily, waiting for the end. She was motionless now, all six hundred feet of her, looming dark against the bleak gray sky. Her skipper, Captain B. J. Rodgers, sent up a flag hoist reading, "My speed zero." It seemed the last message she would ever send. The big Japanese ships could finish her off now as she lay still in the water, and there was hardly a man aboard who did not expect to go down with her.

At that moment Admiral McMorris took the greatest gamble of his life. In a last-ditch effort to save one ship, he would send in three more. But these were the little ships, the destroyers, known to the fleet as "little boys" and certainly no match for the Japanese heavy cruisers. More than likely, they would be blown out of the water before they could even bring their guns to bear. Still, the sheer daring of it might do the trick. And every heavy cruiser at that stage of the war, so soon after the crippling blow at Pearl Harbor, would be worth ten later on. It was a fateful decision for McMorris, a desperate gamble, and he had little time to think about it. He ordered the destroyers forward.

The *Bailey* was first in line. On her bridge, Captain R. S. Riggs received the order to attack and knew that he was going to his death. Yet he could see the justice of it; the *Salt Lake City* must be saved at all costs. He signaled to the other two destroyers, "The targets are the heavies," and then ordered his ship over in a hard turn that rolled her lee rail under and squared her away straight for the enemy, with the other two "little boys" behind.

46

The destroyers seemed to leap forward as the thousands of horsepower of their whining turbines made a muted thunder under their sterns and their propellers sent great rooster tails of spray into the air. The wind roared about them and the smoke from their stacks stood out iron-hard against the lowering sky. They were steaming straight into the guns of the enemy—three little ships against ten, 5,000 tons against 50,000. It was a magnificent, hopeless charge like that of the Light Brigade, lancers racing their speeding horses straight into the mouths of cannon.

On board the *Salt Lake City,* the men waiting for the end were not idle. The ship's guns were still firing, and down in the engine room the black gang was still struggling desperately to contain the inrushing water. Down there in the murderous heat, surrounded by live steam and the thunderous roar of the boilers, the engine-room crew fought their own desperate battle. Only dimly heard was the thunder of the guns from above and the sharp whistle and crack of bursting shells. Inch by inch the water rose while the engineers fought through the maze of pipes and tubes to find the leaks. Shirts and rags were stuffed into cracks. Miraculously, the water rose no higher.

They heard the crescendo of enemy shells burst out with renewed fury as the three destroyers went boring in. Almost at once the "little boys" disappeared into the murk, an apparently hopeless sacrifice. But they were moving so fast that they made difficult targets; the Japa-

47

nese gunners were so startled by the audacious charge that their aim faltered. Long after the war, the captain of the leading Japanese cruiser wrote of the charge of the American destroyers: "I do not know how a ship could live through the concentration of fire that was brought to bear on the leading destroyer."

Yet live on she did, the gallant little *Bailey,* adding the crack of her own 5-inchers to the thunder of the enemy's bigger guns. The three destroyers seemed literally to be smothered with shell splashes. Geysers of foam from the exploding shells rose all about them. And now *Bailey* took the first of four successive hits. An 8-incher went through her thin plating like a bullet going through cardboard and exploded admidships—but still the little ship raced on. Almost at once she was hit again, this time at the waterline, but despite casualties, a hard-working repair crew plugged the gap and the *Bailey* never wavered in her course. Then came a third hit. The engine compartment was flooded and *Bailey* was dead in the water —but not yet finished. For four long tortuous minutes, as shells burst all around her, she lay motionless, a perfect target. And still the Japanese shells missed her. Then an emergency steam supply was gained from the after-boiler and she was building up speed again, 18 knots on the one engine.

She might have turned away with all honor, but that was not the *Bailey*'s style. The amazed Japanese saw her coming in once again, even as the fourth shell hit her straight on. That was the one that should have finished

U.S.S. K. D. Bailey

her, but as it turned out, the shell was a dud that failed to explode. Captain Riggs ordered all torpedoes fired and Lieutenant Commander J. C. Atkeson voiced his ringing "Torpedoes away!" as the five gleaming missiles leaped from their tubes and went sprinting off toward the enemy cruiser *Maya*.

Only seconds later came an additional spread of torpedoes from the two other destroyers, the *Monaghan* and the *Coughlan*. As if that were not enough, the *Salt Lake City* returned to life. The water had been held and even lowered and her engines were back in commission again. She was moving forward, slowly to be sure but under her own power, moving toward the enemy with all guns blazing.

That was too much for Admiral Moshiro Hosogaya on the *Nachi*. With good reason he could ask himself what manner of men he was fighting, what manner of ships. He gave the order to retreat.

No one on board the *Richmond* and *Salt Lake City* knew what had become of the three brave little ships. They had disappeared into the smoke, and the sound of firing had gradually stopped. To those on board the cruisers, it could mean only that the destroyers had been sunk and that the enemy force was now coming on in search of the last of her prey. On board the *Richmond*, they prepared to fight and die.

But then came a message from the *Bailey*—an unbelievable message: "The enemy are retiring to the westward. Shall I follow them?"

50

Panicked by the torpedoes, the ten Japanese ships were scuttling over the horizon as fast as their engines would carry them. A strange silence settled over the gray sea. Even the harsh northern wind had ceased for the moment as the stunned sailors on the American ships tried to understand what had happened—how they had somehow after three and a half hours of bitter fighting against two-to-one odds plucked victory from defeat.

Slowly the exhausted men turned back to their stations as the ships straightened out on a course for home. A drift of fine white snow fanned from the leaden sky. The Battle of the Komandorskis was over.

5   *Flight into Yesterday*

It was raining hard in Lae. Heavy drops of water shivered on the silver wings of the plane, drenching the primitive airstrip, turning the runway to red mud, and sending the natives to the shelter of their grass-roofed huts. It is almost always raining on the coast of New Guinea and this day was no exception. The tall slender woman in coveralls, her hair cropped short, stood gazing disconsolately out at the black squall line sweeping in from the sea. This would mean a delay of at least another twenty-four hours and she chafed at the thought. She had flown halfway around the world—the first woman pilot to attempt an aerial circumnavigation—and with the longest hop ahead, she was seized with impatience to get on with it. At last she shook her head and said, "I guess we'll have to call it off for today, Fred."

Fred Noonan, her navigator, nodded in glum agreement. She was the most experienced woman flier in the world and he respected her judgment.

Slinging her leather flight jacket over her shoulder, Amelia Earhart turned away from the plane and made a dash across the mud to the shelter of the huts. Noonan followed and when they were under cover he spread out his chart of the Pacific. They bent their heads together to take another look at their destination, tiny Howland Island. It would be a flight into yesterday, for they would be crossing the international date line, arriving at Howland the day before they left Lae.

If they arrived at Howland. On the chart, it showed only as the tiniest speck 2,556 miles away in the blue immensity of the Pacific. It would be the most difficult flight Amelia Earhart had ever made. True, she had flown alone across the Atlantic—that had been in 1932, five years to the day after Charles Lindbergh's flight in the *Spirit of St. Louis*—but that had not required nearly the navigational skill or luck needed to hit Howland Island. Flying eastward from New York, one could not help but strike the continent of Europe at some point; in Amelia Earhart's case it had been Londonderry, Ireland. She had landed in Ireland after flying for fifteen hours and eighteen minutes and had climbed through the hatch to find herself the most famous woman flyer of all time.

53

One might have supposed that a solo flight across the Atlantic would have been enough for her. Now, five years later, she was off on a far more hazardous adventure. It was true that this time she had a navigator with her, but even an experienced navigator with the best equipment would have a difficult time finding Howland in any sort of bad weather. And if they did not find Howland, what then? They would be running out of gas in one of the most desolate areas on earth, with only thousands of miles of water ahead. But it would not do to brood about it. This was the way she had chosen and this was the way they must go—into yesterday.

The next morning, July 2, Amelia Earhart's plane, an Electra—overloaded with its 1,150 gallons of gasoline —roared down the runway and clawed its way into the air above Lae. Amelia had flown 22,000 miles to reach New Guinea and had made thirty stops in nineteen countries. She had bucked wind, rain, thunderstorms, and monsoons. But now they were on their way home. After this last, long, dangerous hop, it would all be downhill.

At 2:45 in the morning the radio operator on the U.S. Coast Guard cutter *Itasca* heard Amelia Earhart's voice. Much of what she said was garbled, but the words "cloudy and overcast" were distinctly heard. At 3:45 she was heard again, then again at 6:15, asking for a bearing from the *Itasca,* and then again at 7:42. This time her voice was loud and clear and obviously frantic with worry. "We must be on you," she said, "but cannot see you. Gas is running low. Unable to reach you by radio. We are flying at altitude 1,000 feet."

Amelia Earhart at the controls of her Electra plane.

The weather had closed in again. Visibility was almost nil. At 8:45 Amelia's voice was heard again. "We are running north and south," she said. Those were her last words. Amelia Earhart was never heard from again. She and Fred Noonan disappeared without trace, nor was any wreckage of their plane ever found. The ocean was scoured in the greatest search in history, but Amelia Earhart and Fred Noonan had indeed vanished into yesterday.

One might suppose that the story of Amelia Earhart would have ended with the fruitless search—one more pilot lost at sea on a dangerous overwater flight. But in the years that followed, the legend of Amelia Earhart and the mystery of her disappearance refused to die. Today the mystery is more alive than ever. What could have happened to Amelia Earhart if she did not crash into the sea while searching for Howland Island?

Consider the following facts:

In 1937 this country was not yet at war with Japan, but the Japanese were indeed preparing for war. In violation of the International Mandate laws, they had begun the fortification of certain mid-Pacific islands. Principal among these islands was Truk in the central Carolines. The Carolines had been taken over by Japan in 1920 under a mandate from the League of Nations. Though the terms of the Japanese occupation had specifically stated that the islands would remain unfortified, by the early 1930's it had become clear that something of great

56

significance was happening at Truk. Streams of Japanese freighters and transports were seen heading for Truk in steadily increasing numbers. The natives were held virtual prisoners, but those who did manage to slip away reported that vast fortifications were being erected. The Japanese politely refused all requests that observers be permitted to inspect the island. Since the League of Nations had by that time become powerless, there was nothing anyone could do about it. The only nation directly threatened by such fortifications, the United States, was not eager to provoke an incident with the Japanese. Thus, in early 1937, when Amelia Earhart was planning her round-the-world flight, it was an open secret in the Pacific that Truk was being turned into one of the strongest naval bases in the world.

Is it possible then that the U.S. government asked Amelia Earhart to fly over Truk and take a look around? Does that explain her choice of the difficult cross-Pacific route? Did some American official reason that even if her presence did become known to the Japanese, they would hardly do anything about it? She was, after all, a civilian pilot on a peaceful mission. If she were caught, it would be easy to say she had simply strayed off course. She was the most famous woman flyer in the world; surely the Japanese would not attempt to harm her. Did Amelia Earhart in fact fly over Truk, and was her plane shot down, and was she taken prisoner by the Japanese?

At the end of World War II, Jacqueline Cochran, also a

57

well-known woman flyer, was in Tokyo on a government mission. At the Imperial Air Force Headquarters she saw files containing a great number of references to Amelia Earhart. Those files have since disappeared. They were not among the captured documents recorded by the U.S. government, and the Japanese deny they ever existed.

At the end of the war there lived on the island of Saipan a girl named Josephine Blanco who worked for the United States forces. Josephine told a strange story that a native girl under those circumstances could hardly have invented in such detail. One day in the summer of 1937, as she was riding her bicycle toward Tanapag Harbor, she heard an airplane flying overhead. She looked up and saw a silver, twin-engine plane that appeared to be in trouble. As she watched, the plane came in low over the harbor and crash-landed in the water. By the time Josephine reached the shore, the occupants of the plane had been removed and were standing uninjured, surrounded by Japanese guards. They were a man and a woman, obviously American. The woman was tall and slender and wore a man's clothes and had her hair cut short. Josephine was later shown a picture of Amelia Earhart and Fred Noonan and identified them immediately as the couple she had seen.

Did Amelia and Fred in fact reach Saipan while heading for Howland? The amount of gas they were carrying would have permitted them to stay in the air until about noon. It was just after noon when Josephine Blanco saw the plane go down. Amelia's last message had said she

58

was flying north and south. Saipan was north and west. In their search for Howland, however, they could conceivably have flown as far north as Saipan and crash-landed there. Any stranger landing in Saipan in 1937, particularly an American, would have had little chance of being seen again, especially if he might have flown over Truk and taken pictures. That is one speculation: that Amelia Earhart and Fred Noonan crash-landed on Saipan, were taken prisoner by the Japanese and shot.

Another theory, based on other evidence, is that the round-the-world flight ended not at Saipan but at Mili Atoll in the southeastern Marshalls, a group of islands also held by the Japanese under their League of Nations mandate. Those who hold this theory believe that after the crash Amelia waded ashore and found only a handful of natives on the island, none of whom spoke English. Noonan was injured in the crash, they think, and the natives helped to carry him ashore. Amelia went back to the plane and began to send an SOS signal over her radio, a signal quickly intercepted by the Japanese. While the search for the missing plane was going on over half the Pacific, the Japanese dispatched a boat to Mili to take the fliers to Jaluit, then to Kwajalein, and finally to Saipan, where they either died under torture or were shot.

Neither speculation is based on hard fact; both are largely hearsay and guesswork. But the theories refuse to die even after all these years, and conjectures have enough vitality to keep the mystery alive.

59

U.S. Marines who occupied Saipan during the war claim to have excavated a grave that contained the remains of an American man and woman. Other Marines say that a woman's suitcase, containing clothing, newspaper clippings about Amelia Earhart, and a diary with Amelia Earhart's name engraved on it in gold, was found in a barracks room. The suitcase and diary were turned over to Marine Intelligence and never seen again.

Were Amelia Earhart and Fred Noonan in fact on a secret spying mission for the U.S. government, and has there been a conspiracy of silence regarding their disappearance? The government has officially denied sending Amelia on a mission over Truk, but several prominent military men and U.S. Senators—among them the late Admiral Nimitz, who was commander in chief of the Pacific fleet during the war—believed that there was more to the story than was ever revealed, and encouraged newspapermen who were puzzling over Amelia Earhart's disappearance to go on with the search. Certainly Admiral Nimitz was an intelligent man, and certainly his loyalty to the government is beyond question, yet even he seemed to feel that the entire story had never been told and that certain vital records had disappeared.

Amelia Earhart and Fred Noonan are unquestionably long since dead—whether on Saipan, in a Japanese prison, or in the wreckage of their plane in the deep blue waters off Howland Island—but the how and why of their mysterious end have refused to die with them.

6 *The Nine Lives of Lieutenant Miller*

He moved out of the brush as cautiously as a frightened turtle sticks its head out of its shell. The beach, shimmering under the rays of the South Pacific sun, stretched out in blinding whiteness. It seemed empty but the man took no chances. Very slowly he parted the leaves in front of him and studied the beach, yard by yard, before making another move.

A giant land crab caught his eye. It came out of its hole in the coral and moved toward the water. The man watched it carefully for two reasons. First, it made an

61

excellent sentinel because it was sensitive to vibration and would scurry back to its hole if alarmed by the approach of a patrol. Second, the man was desperately in need of food and intended to eat that crab.

Sweat trickled down his arms and onto his rifle. Thirsty as he was, he could hardly believe there was any moisture left in his body, but still the sweat came. A mosquito buzzed angrily about his ear and then stabbed his neck. The man made no effort to brush it away; he could not risk the sudden motion that would attract the notice either of the crab or of any human eye that might be observing the beach and the jungle beyond.

There was no sound, no breeze; not a leaf stirred. Behind him a parrot screeched, and the sudden sound so tore at his taut nerves that despite himself he jumped slightly. At last, satisfied that the beach was indeed empty, he slid the rifle out onto the sand in front of him and let his head and shoulders follow.

The rifle was Japanese and the man wore a Japanese uniform, but he was unmistakably American. The uniform, which had been made for a much smaller man, was strained to bursting by his big shoulders. The little Japanese service cap looked almost ludicrous atop his gaunt, bronzed face. And when he stood erect it could be seen that although emaciated, he still had the powerful build of a football player.

His name was Lieutenant Hugh Barr Miller. Until two weeks before, he had been a deck officer on the United

62

States destroyer *Strong.* The year was 1943 and the place was Arundel Island in the Solomons. How he had come there is an amazing story of survival perhaps unequaled in all the long and bloody history of World War II.

On the night of July 4 the *Strong* had been part of a task force consisting of three light cruisers and three other destroyers bound for Visuvisu Point, the northern tip of the Japanese-held island of New Georgia. It was their mission to bombard enemy fortifications and clear a way for an American landing.

By midnight the task force under the command of Admiral W. L. Ainsworth was well up into the "Slot," a narrow strait where American and Japanese ships had been hammering at each other for months. There was just enough moonlight to impart a faint, almost phosphorescent visibility. Although there had been a radar report of unidentified vessels sometime earlier, there had as yet been no evidence of enemy activity. The ships bored steadily northward through the night, when suddenly a lookout on the bridge of the *Strong* saw the ghostly white wake of a torpedo rushing toward them. His cry of "Torpedo!" came too late. A moment later there was a thunder blast on the port side as the ship was struck amidship.

The torpedo which struck *Strong* burst her hull as it would a melon. The blast wiped out her forward fireroom and water came rushing into the hull, flooding the engine room. The bodies of men killed in the blast were hurled forward on the tide of black water. Others, wounded and dying, could be heard moaning for help in the unlit compartments.

As soon as Admiral Ainsworth saw that *Strong* had been torpedoed, he ordered two other destroyers to rush to her assistance. The ship could never be saved, but it was still possible to get survivors off. Unfortunately, at that moment, the enemy shore gunners at Enogai Inlet became aware of what had happened. The ship and her rescuers were illuminated in a red glare, and at once the Japanese guns opened up. A salvo of shells bracketed the already stricken ship.

As shells burst all about them, the rescue ships bravely closed in beside the *Strong*. One of them, *Chevalier,* thrust her bow straight into the wreckage and thereby suffered some damage herself but was able to provide a web of nets and lines on which the more severely wounded men were handed across. The sea was calm. *Chevalier* might have gotten them all away had not the enemy gunners on the beach maintained so deadly a fire.

As it was, *Chevalier* did take off about 240 of the *Strong*'s crew, but after having stayed alongside for some seven minutes under enemy fire her commander felt that he could no longer risk his ship. As *Chevalier* pulled away, two more shells landed on *Strong*'s deck, blowing several wounded men into the water.

The *Strong,* ablaze and torn into steel fragments, went down at twenty-two minutes past one o'clock in the morning. Yet even then the explosions which had racked her did not end, for as she sank, several of the 300-pound depth charges she had carried on deck exploded in the water, further maiming or killing the unfortunate men still afloat beside the sinking ship.

Among those injured by the undersea blasts was Lieutenant Hugh Miller. Although barely conscious and very badly hurt, he managed to tread water and remain afloat. In a huddle around him were some twenty-three men clinging to life nets and pieces of raft. The moon was down now and the night was so black that it would have been virtually impossible for any of the rescuing ships to find them. Besides, a strong current was moving them steadily away from their shipmates and the spot where the *Strong* had gone down.

Morning found the survivors drifting in an empty world of gulf and sky and burning sun. Somehow they clung to the wreckage which supported them, but their holds grew steadily weaker. One by one they slipped away. Among the wounded who would not let go was Lieutenant Miller. He had been an All-American quarterback at the University of Alabama and perhaps it was this rugged training in a bruising sport that gave him the grit to hang on. Or perhaps it was simply that the spark of life burned brighter in him than it does in most men, a spark that refused to be extinguished.

Day after day the men, who were now almost as lifeless as the flotsam upon which they floated, drifted across the sea. During the day the fierce sun scorched them and at night they shivered under driving squalls. The only

65

water they had was what they could lick from their parched lips as sheets of rain slashed down at them. Finally, after four days of agony, they were washed ashore on Arundel Island, midway between New Georgia and Kolombangara. Of the twenty-three who had originally clung to the wreckage, only six remained. Among them was Lieutenant Miller.

Two of the six died of their injuries after crawling ashore. That left the lieutenant and three sailors. Together they tried to work their way through the jungle, but Miller was so weakened by internal bleeding caused by the depth-charge explosions that it did not seem he could live much longer. On July 14, ten days after the ship had gone down, he suffered a massive hemorrhage. When he regained consciousness, Miller was convinced that he was dying. He told the three sailors to leave him and try to reach friendly territory. When they refused, he gave his last official order: they were to leave him where he lay. At last they agreed.

He ordered them to take the rest of the emergency rations, his shoes, and any of his clothing that might be useful. The only thing he kept for himself was a broken pocketknife. Reluctantly, they stripped Miller naked and left him to die. He sank back into a condition of semiconsciousness and waited for the end.

But the end did not come. Although the spark of life flickered like a candle in the wind, it did not quite go out. On the afternoon of the seventeenth, a tropical downpour revived Miller. He gulped a few swallows of

66

rain water and dragged himself to his feet. Blindly he staggered off through the jungle toward the beach.

Movement was agony. His bare feet were shredded by the coral, and the sun blistered his shoulders. He limped on with no real objective and hardly any hope, simply obeying the urge to survive. So weak was he that often he stumbled and fell full-length. The green world of the jungle seemed to swim around him in a watery haze and he was drenched every now and then by a short swift tropical downpour. When that happened, he licked his lips to relieve his thirst and noticed for the first time the absence of the taste of blood in his mouth. The internal bleeding, which had so nearly killed him, had somehow stopped of its own accord.

That night it rained again and Miller lay motionless in the yellow mud while the rain beat down on his unprotected head. He suffered from chills and knew that he was racked with fever, but in the morning the fever was gone. He felt cooler and a little stronger. That afternoon he found a coconut and, using his bit of newfound strength, managed to crack it open and eat the meat. At first he thought he would be sick, but he managed by an effort of will to keep the nourishing white meat of the nut in his stomach, the first food he had eaten in more than two weeks.

At nightfall the driving rains came again, but this time Miller had the energy to gather up a dozen or so palm fronds and erect a shelter of sorts over his head. In the morning he felt better than at any time since he had

67

come to Arundel Island and ate another coconut and a red melon-like fruit, which he hacked open with his broken knife.

The next day he felt considerably stronger and was able to get through the jungle at a good pace. He moved down to the beach to wash his torn feet in salt water in the hope that the coral cuts would not fester. Suddenly his eye was caught by something half buried in the sand. He tugged at it and unearthed a Japanese army blanket. Curious as to what a blanket was doing on the beach, Miller scouted a little farther up toward the brush and came suddenly upon the body of a man—a Japanese soldier lying face down, still clutching his rifle. Miller guessed that the dead man had been washed ashore from one of the Japanese transports sunk in the night battles in the Slot.

Quickly he stripped off the dead man's clothing, took his rifle and ammunition pouches, and scuttled away into the brush. Lying motionless in the brush, his heart pounding, Miller waited to see if he had been observed. Nothing stirred. The screeching of the birds went on without pause. Satisfied at last that no enemy patrol was about to pounce on him, Miller dressed in the Japanese uniform and then cleaned the rifle. Despite the exposure to salt water and sand, it was still in working order. He reloaded the clip with fresh bullets and then examined the rest of his newly acquired equipment. In the ammunition pouch were two hand grenades and some small cans of emergency rations. He broke open the cans and ate the food. When he stood up this time, he was no longer Hugh Miller, the hopeless castaway. He was once again Lieutenant Miller, armed and fed, a one-man army.

On August 5 he observed a Japanese patrol working along the beach. He watched them carefully from the brush. It seemed obvious that they had found the soldier's body and were on the hunt for the person who had stripped him. They worked along the beach and through the edge of the jungle. Suddenly one of them observed a footprint in the sand and, beyond that, other prints which led toward the American's hiding place. In an excited voice he shouted something which brought the rest of the patrol clustering around him. At that moment Lieutenant Miller rose from his hiding place and with the same easy motion which had once sent touchdown passes winging into the end zone tossed a grenade in among them. Almost at once he followed it with another.

When the smoke and flame had cleared, the five Japanese were sprawled lifeless. Miller quickly stripped them of weapons and supplies and then moved away into the jungle.

Thus began what was perhaps the strangest aspect of this already almost unbelievable story of survival. Lieutenant Miller took the offensive. He built himself a little lean-to shelter in the jungle and established it as his headquarters. In another place nearby, he cached his weapons and supplies. Then he set out to locate and raid the enemy base.

He could not of course launch any sort of frontal assault on the Japanese base, but he could lurk in the jungle and ambush stragglers and small patrols. The Japanese tried everything from native scouts to dogs in an effort to pin him down, but each time he slipped away. With apparent ease, he ran and struck and slipped away again from the enemy. It was a devastating performance. Try as they did, the enemy simply could not pin down this wolf-like creature that harassed them with such ferocity.

And if Lieutenant Miller's actions were wolf-like, so too was his appearance. He had lost forty pounds and was down to bone and sinew. Pale blue eyes burned out of his face, the lower half of which was covered by a reddish beard. In the struggle for survival, all his senses had been sharpened to the point where he could hear an enemy patrol approaching while it was still hundreds of yards away. And if he did not hear it himself, he could tell from the suddenly muted voices of the birds and monkeys that danger was approaching.

Although the odds were fantastically unequal, Lieutenant Miller enjoyed one advantage that went beyond his own strength and determination: he was absolutely alone, so he knew that any approaching force could only belong to the enemy. Thus he was constantly on the alert and prepared to strike regardless of the situation. When the Japanese sent out encircling patrols, he was able to slip through with comparative ease because the enemy often hesitated for fear of firing on their own men.

Miller had now been forty-three days on Arundel Island and was stronger and better armed than ever. In his various forays and ambushes he had killed more than thirty enemy soldiers and collected a valuable store of information regarding enemy troop movements and positions on the island. But each day the odds against his survival grew greater. The situation had become intolerable to the Japanese commander and he was committing constantly larger forces to the pursuit and destruction of the harasser. Miller was aware that his string was being played out. He still managed to outmaneuver the patrols that were searching for him, but each time the margin of escape became narrower. He no longer dared risk the sound of gunfire; when he killed, he had to do it with his hands or with a knife. His lean-to shelter had long since been destroyed and he no longer dared return to the area where he had hidden his supplies.

On the forty-third day, Miller had a marvelous stroke of luck. He was searching the beach at low water for crabs when he saw an American seaplane flying slowly along the coast. Although he had often seen friendly planes at a distance, it was the first time one had ever approached so close.

In a moment he had torn off the enemy tunic, thrown away his rifle, and rushed down to the water's edge. This was a great gamble, for if a Japanese patrol had caught up with him at that moment he would have been helpless. But it was a chance he could not pass up. Miller dashed into the water and scampered up and down waving his arms. The plane went by and he watched it with

71

Lt. Hugh Barr Miller in November 1943, about three months after he was rescued from Arundel Island.

a sinking heart. But then it turned and came back. They had seen him! In a frenzy of joy he jumped and shouted and rolled in the water. The plane returned and circled over him and he could make out the pilot staring down at him. Despite his bizarre appearance, he knew that his size and build and red hair would clearly identify him as an American.

The pilot had made his decision. The seaplane's hull cleaved an arrow on the calm water and then began to taxi in toward the beach. Powerful arms flailing the water, Miller swam out to meet it. In a moment they had pulled him aboard and were circling out to sea again. Twenty minutes later Lieutenant Hugh Barr Miller, the man who had survived everything, was safe at an American base.

7 The Man Who Cast Himself Away

The yellow rubber raft floated slowly westward. Its solitary occupant, gaunt and bearded, stared out at the heaving horizon. Then he turned to look back at the great gray combers rolling up astern. Nothing. Not a ship, not a bird. Only the endlessly rushing seas.

Now in mid-Atlantic, he had been alone on the raft for thirty days. Presumably it would take him another thirty days to reach land somewhere in the West Indies. He had no food or water, but he did not despair, for the astonishing thing about this man was that he was the first castaway in history to have placed himself in such a position voluntarily. The year was 1952 and Alain Bombard, a young French physician, was deliberately exposing himself to a hideous death in order to prove a scientific theory: that a man set adrift in a raft could cross the ocean living only on fish and sea water.

This was not the voyage of a madman or publicity seeker. Bombard was serious about his experiment. The need for it had come to him one morning a year or two before when he was the house surgeon at a small hospital on the French coast. He had been awakened by a report that a fishing trawler had missed her course during the night and had piled up on the outer end of a rocky breakwater. The survivors would need medical attention.

But there were no survivors. There had been forty-three men on board and now there were forty-three dead men piled on the beach like so much driftwood, each still wearing his life jacket. A split-second error of navigation had cost the lives of forty-three men and left seventy-eight orphans.

Bombard was appalled. He began to look into the incidence of shipwrecks along the French coast and the ratio of fatalities. He discovered that one town alone, Boulogne, lost between a hundred and a hundred fifty fishermen each year. Researching further, he discovered that throughout the world in peacetime more than 200,000 men and women suffered the same fate every year. That was an amazing figure, but even more astonishing was the fact that more than a quarter of those who died did not die in the sea. They died in lifeboats after having survived the threat of drowning.

Why did 50,000 people die each year in lifeboats, and what could be done to save them?

Doctor Bombard's research seemed to indicate that castaways died not only from privation but from fear. Could a man actually die of despair? Among the classic examples is that of the frigate *La Méduse,* lost in 1816 on a sandbank a hundred miles off the African coast. There were 149 survivors—passengers, soldiers, and a few officers—who trusted themselves to a hastily constructed raft towed by the ship's boats. On the raft were six barrels of wine and two of water. The tow broke and the raft drifted at sea for twelve days before being sighted by a ship. By that time there were only fifteen survivors, ten of whom died shortly after being rescued.

Why had so many died? Twelve days at sea on an open raft is certainly a terrible ordeal, but it should not account for so many deaths. And they had not died of thirst, for if the wine and water had been carefully rationed there would have been enough to maintain life. Nor had they died of starvation; it has been demonstrated repeatedly that the human body can survive for much longer periods without food. The great Indian leader Gandhi proved that by his fasts, as did Captain Bligh, who lived for forty-eight days in an open boat on eight days' provisions.

What was it then that had kept Gandhi and Bligh alive while so many of the castaways on the raft had died? It

76

could hardly be physical strength, for Gandhi was almost incredibly frail even before he began his fasts. Perhaps then it had to do with moral fiber. Gandhi was seeking to free his country from foreign rule and, buoyed up by that hope, he was able to survive conditions that would have killed another man. Bligh was as strongly motivated (although in his case it was by a thirst for revenge against the mutineers), and he was determined to survive and reach England. The answer then must be that despair had helped to kill the men on the raft.

A perfect example of how despair and panic can kill occurred many years later when the world's largest steamship, the *Titanic,* struck an iceberg in the North Atlantic. The first relief ships arrived less than three hours after the great ship had gone down; yet in that brief period a number of people had either died or gone mad in the lifeboats. To put it plainly, they had died of fear. Yet no child under the age of ten had died. The children, unlike their elders, had not succumbed to hysteria.

Bombard went on to additional research and always came up with the same answer. Ninety percent of the survivors of shipwreck die within three days, yet we all know that it takes longer than that to perish of hunger and thirst. What happens in the mind of a man whose ship goes down? Without a deck under his feet, he is suddenly overwhelmed by fear—fear of sea and wind and solitude and hunger and thirst. Yet if the same man could be convinced that his situation was not hopeless—that the sea itself provided the stuff of life—could he not survive a great deal longer, with a far better chance of rescue?

Bombard then began to do serious research into the life-giving properties of sea water. He discovered that there are nearly two hundred times as many living organisms in a cubic yard of water as in the same amount of earth, and that a moderate amount of salt water taken slowly and carefully will support life. But how could one convince those people who might some day be shipwrecked that all this was not just textbook theory but really true?

The only way, Bombard decided, was to subject himself to the worst possible conditions a shipwrecked man might encounter and to subsist entirely off the sea, with no outside aid. He could do it in a laboratory, but that would convince no one; his laboratory must be the sea itself. He would set himself adrift like any survivor—and not just for a few days. To get his message across, he must subject himself to the hardest, longest, most difficult and dangerous voyage any shipwrecked man had ever made. He would go alone across the Atlantic without any food or water except what he could get from the sea.

The vessel in which Bombard proposed to make this voyage was as strange as the voyage itself. It was nothing more than a horseshoe-shaped, inflatable rubber sausage fifteen feet long and six feet wide. The open end was closed by a wooden stern board over which he would be able to trail fishing nets and lines without causing dam-

L'Hérétique before the transatlantic journey. Alain Bombard is at left, his friend and consultant at right.

age by friction to the fragile rubber floats. The bottom of the boat was three feet wide and carried a lightweight wooden deck board on which the solitary passenger would do his living. He had named his boat, appropriately, *L'Hérétique—The Nonbeliever*.

Attempting to cross the ocean in so unlikely a vessel was not quite as absurd as it seemed. For one thing, there was not a single piece of metal in the whole construction, and the floats were divided into five airtight compartments, which meant that even if one or two of them were to be punctured, the craft itself would remain afloat. And there was an outside valve which could be turned on and off as required, allowing air to pass from one compartment to another, thus permitting Bombard to replenish the air from a bellows pump. The boat had a small mast and a tiny sail about three yards square. Though the boat would not sail into the wind at all and the sail could be used only when running off, the voyage would be made in the trade winds, presumably always with a fair wind, so the sail would be useful. Over the bows was a rubberized sheet under which Bombard could crawl for shelter.

Now came the question of a choice of route. The shortest way in terms of miles would have been to go straight westward, but that would have posed two major problems. To the north lay the Sargasso Sea, some five thousand miles in diameter. This area is known to contain great masses of seaweed but little else. It has been said that no edible fish has ever been caught there, and since Bombard was relying entirely upon fish for food, he could not afford to take such a risk. Like many landsmen, he was prone to believe the wild tales circulated about the Sargasso Sea—that any ship which sails into it will be caught in an unbreakable grip by the plant tendrils and seaweed and will circle helplessly until it rots and sinks. Those who have actually sailed in the Sargasso Sea know that, while it does contain a high proportion of weed, the weed itself would never be thick enough to trap a vessel.

Bombard also wanted to avoid an equally unattractive area of uncertain winds to the south known as the Doldrums. Therefore he would be like a man walking down a dark street at night with enemies on either side; all he could do was stay in the middle and hope for the best.

And so Bombard was ready at last for the great experiment. If the truth be told, his heart was not in it. He was no sailor and he dreaded the long voyage alone in the little boat. How would he stand the monotony, the boredom, the loneliness? Well, how did any castaway stand it? That was what he must determine if his experiment was to be of value.

No matter what his misgivings, Bombard had made up his mind to go through with it. It was like any other experiment, he told himself, basically a matter of organization. But this time, instead of test tubes and microscopes, his tools would be a fish press to extract fresh water from the fish he caught, a sea anchor to hold the bow of the rubber boat up into the wind during gales, and a very

81

fine mesh net with which to extract plankton from the sea.

The day of his departure was reasonably calm and pleasant. *L'Hérétique* moved along easily before the following wind. But the second day the wind increased and by the third night it was blowing a gale. Great waves were breaking all around him. Bombard could not help but wonder what would happen if one of these onrushing waterfalls should break directly on him. Despite his fear and the violent motion of the boat, he managed to fall asleep, only to find himself in what at first appeared to be a nightmare. As if in a dream, he seemed to be overwhelmed by water. Confused and panic-stricken, he tried to gather his thoughts. Was there still a boat under him? Was he in the boat or in the water? He started swimming, striking out desperately. At last, half dead with fright, he was completely awake. It was no dream. *L'Hérétique* was half submerged. While he slept, a wave had broken right on top of the boat.

Bombard started bailing desperately, using his hat and hands and anything else he could find, but every ten or fifteen minutes another crest hit the stern board with a thud and put back as much water as he had been able to remove. All the same he persisted and at last, after two hours of violent work, managed to get the dinghy properly afloat again. The experience was a lesson to Bombard and to all other castaways. Persist and you can win. Be more obstinate than the sea and the sea will relent.

The boat had survived the worst conditions it was ever

82

likely to encounter, but much of Bombard's equipment had been ruined by sea water. Even more important, his morale was low. He had been made sharply aware of just how vulnerable his fragile craft was to wind and weather. He was now truly in the position of the castaway—chattering with cold, soaked to the skin, and exhausted. These conditions in turn made him weak and fearful. And it was fear, he knew, that would prove more deadly than the elements.

He waited desperately for the sun to rise. Darkness is the great ally of fear. In the dark the seas seem twice as big, the cold more intense, the loneliness more oppressive. He had to get a grip on himself, for ahead lay fifty or sixty such nights of fearful loneliness. If he could not conquer his panic, he would not survive them.

Waiting for daylight at sea seems endless. The minutes drag by like hours. One looks to the eastern sky for some faint glow, some glimmer of light, but sees instead only the racing clouds and the swiftly obscured stars. Even moonlight gives courage and strength to the man at sea, but that night there was no moon. The long hours dragged by. Many times Bombard considered turning back, giving up. But there was no way back. His tiny sail was a help in running before the wind, but there was no way in the world that he could sail his boat against the wind, and the wind was taking him ever farther out into the great Atlantic. He was committed now, as every castaway is committed, and he had to see it through.

A thousand times that night Bombard cursed himself for a fool. He thought of his wife and their comfortable home and asked himself what mania had possessed him to leave it for this. No one, after all, had forced him into this position. Even if he were to survive, what could he gain by it? There was no pot of gold at the end of the rainbow. He might go mad with fear and arrive fit only for an asylum. Who was he to think that he could challenge this monstrous ocean and win? His scientific zeal had blinded him to the terrible reality of the cruel sea and what it could do to a man alone.

Yet, when the sun at last rose, Bombard's spirits began to rise with it. He busied himself cleaning the boat, restowing his wet gear, drying his matches, sewing the torn sail. These activities made him feel stronger, more in control. And to his surprise and delight he found the raft surrounded by fish darting around him like green jewels in the blue water. It was high time to start laying in a supply.

All day he busied himself, bending the point of his knife very gently so as to form a sort of harpoon. When he had shaped it to his satisfaction, he bound it to the handle of an oar, using for that purpose only what might be available to a castaway—a necktie, shoelace, or belt. Although he carried an emergency fishing kit, he was determined to use only what might be available to the average man suddenly cast away on a raft.

While Bombard was working on the harpoon, he no-

84

ticed several birds overhead. This surprised him, since he had been told by experts that he would not see any birds once he was out of sight of land. The fact was that he saw birds on every day of the trip, and many of the same ones seemed to stay with him throughout the voyage.

The same was true of fish. Fish were essential to his whole plan; without them, he could not hope to survive. Yet the experts had advised him that there were no fish far out at sea. Fish hugged the reefs and coastal areas, they said; once he had left Europe, he would not see fish again until he approached the West Indies. But there were all the fish he wanted, circling around him, apparently attracted to the raft and utilizing it for shade and protection.

Bombard's first attempts at spearing fish were futile. He struck them with his harpoon but managed only to wound them and see them wriggle off. At last, on the second day of trying, he managed to spear his first dolphin and drag it on board. To his surprise, the other fish did not dash away but stayed as before, close around the raft. This, as Bombard was to discover, is the way with dolphin. It was a great boost to his courage. He felt that he was saved. By squeezing the fish in a press, he could extract enough liquid to take the place of fresh water. He would then dry the body of the fish in the sun, thus laying in a ready food supply. In addition, he found a perfect natural bone hook behind the gill cover of the dolphin—precisely the same kind of bone hook one finds

85

in the tombs of prehistoric men. Bombard no longer had to risk his precious knife using it as a harpoon. With the bone hook he could catch all the fish he needed.

Bombard now had an experience which is common to all who embark on long ocean voyages alone: time began to lose its meaning. Only night and day reminded him of the passage of time. Otherwise, the days merged into each other in a sort of dreamlike sequence. The second week out, he celebrated his twenty-eighth birthday. His birthday present to himself that day was the capture of a sea bird which had swooped down and swallowed his fishhook. Bombard divided the bird in half and ate one half, raw. That night he noticed a curious thing: the remaining portion of the sea bird was giving out a phosphorescent glow so strong that it cast a light on his sail, giving the whole boat a ghostly appearance.

It was at this point in his voyage that Bombard decided to put himself on a strict schedule of activities. It was no good for a castaway simply to let himself drift passively at the mercy of the elements; he must somehow manage to convince himself that he remained the master of what was happening to him. Under his new program, Bombard rose at dawn and collected the flying fish which had fallen into the boat during the night, usually between five and fifteen. He ate two for breakfast and put the others aside. Then he fished for an hour, catching a dolphin or two which would provide him with food and liquid for the rest of the day.

After fishing, he would devote an hour to a scrupulous

inspection of the boat, checking any spot where chafe might have started. Anything that rubbed against the rubberized canvas was a potential hazard, and this need to keep the fragile skin of the boat intact was one of the greatest problems of the voyage. Bombard would run his fingers carefully over the entire surface in order to detect any roughness.

Then came half an hour of exercise to keep himself supple, after which he would drink two coffee cups of sea water with plankton. The plankton, caught in the fine mesh net that trailed behind the boat, supplied him with enough vitamin C to ward off scurvy. At noon he would take sights with his sextant, and in the afternoon he would read or write if the weather permitted. At two o'clock every day he gave himself a complete physical checkup, including blood pressure and temperature. All these facts were carefully recorded in his log. In the evening he gave himself another medical examination and noted any changes from the afternoon.

By this time Bombard had been at sea for twenty days. He had lost weight, was growing weaker and more fearful. He spoke aloud in order to hear the sound of his own voice, and filled page after page in his diary since it gave him the illusion of another presence on board. Like a man awaiting release from prison, he checked off each day and told himself that if all went well he would reach land in ten more days, an estimate based on what he assumed to be an accurate navigational fix. What he did not know—and could not possibly have known at the time—

was that his watch was no longer keeping accurate time and that his plotted positions for longitude were entirely wrong. He told himself each day that he was very nearly there, but he was actually only halfway across and still had another thirty days at sea.

One wonderful thing happened to him at that point. It rained! On November 11 the clouds opened and he was submerged in torrents of fresh water, the first he had drunk in more than three weeks. His skin soaked it in. The fact that Bombard had proved conclusively that he could live for three weeks without fresh water in no way diminished his enjoyment of this unexpected bath. He drank until he could hold no more and then stored the rest in containers. From that day on, he always had enough rain water to meet his requirements.

But everything else seemed to go wrong. Squalls roared overhead. Once more he was flooded and half sunk. To add to his other troubles, his physical condition was beginning to deteriorate. His whole body was covered with small red lumps, and even the skin under his fingernails was inflamed and painful to the touch. Pockets of pus formed under his nails and he had to lance them without anesthetic. Constant immersion in water was causing the skin to peel from his feet in great strips. He had completely lost the nails from four toes and was facing the serious possibility of gangrene. It was a time when he might easily have given way to despair.

To take his mind off his condition, Bombard dove overboard to inspect the bottom of his boat and there

88

found something even more alarming. Whole colonies of barnacles had formed along the seams of the rubber floats. Not only did these reduce his speed, but there was every likelihood that their hard shells would pierce the rubber. If that happened, he was finished. His situation was becoming desperate.

And now the wind died. The boat lay motionless day after day under a terrible sun. Bombard's rubber shelter cloth had long since been carried away, and even his hat was gone. He wrapped a scrap of cloth around his head but it did very little to shield him from the sun. He began to think of death and on that day, December 6, wrote out his will.

Yet even if his raft some day drifted ashore with only a skeleton on board, it would not prove that he had failed. He had already survived four weeks on the open sea, an ordeal far greater than that imposed on the average castaway. He still kept a meticulous log, but his handwriting was no longer legible. A fantasy of magnificent meals and marvelous wines flashed through his mind. He wrote down the menu that he would like to have ordered for his last meal on earth.

On his fifty-third day at sea he saw a ship—a large passenger liner some miles off but on a converging course. He fumbled feverishly for his mirror and tried to flash the reflected rays of the sun toward the ship. At last he was seen and the ship changed course to approach him.

When they were alongside, Bombard asked for his

exact position. The answer stunned him. For the past week he had supposed that he was only forty to fifty miles from land and that at any moment he would sight a mountain top on one of the islands. Now he discovered that his navigation had been wrong. He was six hundred miles from his estimated position. Six hundred miles! He sagged as though struck with a hammer.

"Will you come aboard?" asked the captain of the ship.

Bombard could only nod. It was too much. He was finished. He could not possibly survive another six hundred miles. He would have them hoist the raft on board and he himself would get into a comfortable bed in a cool cabin. The nightmare voyage was over.

Then all the agony of the past six weeks came back to him. Was it all to be for nothing? If he stayed on the liner, the world would remember only that he had failed. He must go on even if he died in the attempt. It was the hardest decision of his life. In the end Bombard asked to be put back on his raft.

The days of torture crawled by. On the afternoon of December 21 he hailed another ship and again asked for his position. This time the news was much better. He was now only seventy miles from the north coast of Barbados. The wind was pushing him along at good speed and it was just possible that he might see the flash of a lighthouse sometime that night. This time he had no inclination to board the ship. The end was in sight and he must hurry on.

And that night he did see the light, the first indication

L'Hérétique on the beach at Barbados, after the sixty-two-day transatlantic journey.

of land he had seen in sixty-five days. His spirits soared.

In the morning the magnificently green island was clearly visible. Almost mad with happiness and expectation, Bombard steered the raft toward an opening in the reef. Twenty minutes later *L'Hérétique* grated on the sand. The gaunt, weakened, ragged, but indestructible Dr. Bombard stumbled out onto the sand and managed to hold himself erect as the natives ran toward him.

8 *Tzu Hang*

Tzu Hang may be the luckiest ship in the world—with the unluckiest crew. Or it may be the other way around. In any case, *Tzu Hang* survived an ordeal never before recorded in all the long history of man's ventures upon the water. And she survived it not once but twice.

Her owner was Miles Smeeton, a former British army officer. Like most army people, General Smeeton did not know very much about the water when he bought *Tzu Hang*. But he thought she looked shippy. It was an amazingly well-informed choice for a man who had never sailed a boat. *Tzu Hang* was a 46-foot teakwood ketch built in Hong Kong. She looked as though she

93

could go around the world, and that was what the Smeetons (Miles, his wife Beryl, and their eleven-year-old
daughter Clio) decided to do. Now the average individual will think a long time before deciding to go around
the world in a small sailboat, and when he has thought
about it long enough he is usually too old to do anything
about it. But the Smeetons were a different breed. What
they thought about, they did. And so after one trial trip
across the English Channel to learn how to sail the con-
founded thing, off they went. Miles and Beryl handled
the sailing, navigating and cooking, while Clio and the
cat took care of the rest. With typical British understate-
ment, they made about as much fuss over their departure
as you and I would make about taking the car out for
a Sunday afternoon spin.

All went well on the merry ship *Tzu Hang*. They
crossed the South Atlantic to Panama and then went
through the canal and on up the west coast of the United
States to Vancouver, British Columbia. From there they
eventually made their way to Australia.

So far it had all been, as the English say, a piece of
cake. They'd had their share of storms, of course, but
Tzu Hang had behaved beautifully in even the worst
weather, and the Smeetons had learned to have confidence in their boat and in themselves. Even the cat had
developed into a first-rate sailor who never got sick in
the worst sea. As for Clio, she would not have traded
Tzu Hang for a castle in Scotland. What other eleven-

year-old-girl was going around the world in the family home?

But in Australia some new decisions were made. Clio would have to go back to school in England, and her parents would go on without her. This decision met with considerable resistance from Clio, but at last she agreed. Miles, Beryl, and the cat went sailing off, this time for the greatest voyage of all, a journey around Cape Horn, the dreaded no-man's-land of deep-water voyaging.

Now there are, of course, other ways in which to sail around the world. None is easy, but not all of them are especially dangerous. The voyage around Cape Horn, in the track of the old square-riggers, is certainly the most dangerous of all.

The brooding fist of rock at the end of the long arm of South America is battered day and night, year in and year out, by the fierce westerly winds and the great seas that sweep unimpeded from the Antarctic. The surprising thing is that under such a pounding there is any land left. But the land is still there and the great seas are still there, and the fierce gray cold. If you have to go around the world, there is no harder way of doing it.

It has been done before, but not often. Old Josh Slocum, the first of the singlehanders, did it, but in the years that have followed, fewer than a dozen small yachts have duplicated his feat. Now Miles and Beryl and the cat would attempt it.

In the end there was another man on board, and if

they had searched the world over, it would have been hard to find a more suitable companion for so hazadous a voyage. He was a young Englishman named John Guzzwell, who had already distinguished himself by sailing halfway around the world alone on a small yacht he had built himself. Apart from his obvious qualifications as a seaman, John had one other great attribute. He was a ship's carpenter of the highest order. This skill would prove very valuable to the crew of the *Tzu Hang*.

The first stage of the voyage, from Australia south and east to New Zealand across the Tasman Sea, went well enough, but the real test, the ominous Roaring Forties, still lay ahead. These are the forty degrees of south latitude, presumably so called because of the fierce and incessant roaring of the wind in a boat's rigging.

As *Tzu Hang* drove south, the weather got steadily worse, but they had been expecting that. *Tzu Hang* had already demonstrated her ability to ride out rough weather at sea. During the worst of the storms the ketch lay hove to—that is, under a small storm trysail—and riding comfortably a few points off the wind while her crew stayed below until the worst was over. At no point were they seriously worried. They had plenty of time and plenty of food. Beryl had provisioned the ship from the Smeetons' own farm in Canada. They had all sorts of canned and bottled meats as well as jars of plums, pears, apples, strawberries, and apricots. In even the foulest weather Beryl proved herself a superb ship's cook, and the two men and the cat never had cause to complain of the food.

They were now forty-seven days out and had done close to five thousand miles, almost a fifth of the way around the world. The seas were mountainous. The Smeetons and Guzzwell had of course seen big seas before, but never anything like this. John Guzzwell, an adventurous soul if ever there was one, said the seas could hardly come too big for him, but when the wave tops reached higher than their masthead, which was fifty-six feet above the deck, even John was ready to call it quits.

At that time, shortly after daybreak, they were running under bare poles and dragging 360 feet of heavy rope astern in an effort to slow the yacht down, but even so, *Tzu Hang* was moving too fast. Miles briefly considered heaving to—that is, bringing the bow up into the wind—but the maneuver seemed too dangerous under the conditions then prevailing. It was decided to carry on until there was a lull in the storm.

At nine o'clock in the morning Beryl took over the helm. Only one woman in a million would so much as venture out on deck in such conditions, let alone attempt to steer a boat. But there was no question about Beryl's courage, and Miles had absolute faith in her ability to handle the boat.

Beryl had always loved the challenge of a storm. She was smiling as she went on deck wearing her yellow oilskin trousers, green oilskin coat, a pair of John's sea boots, and woolen mittens. She wore a life line around

97

her waist, the snap shackled to one of the masthead shrouds.

For as long as Miles Smeeton lives, he will never forget what happened next. He was lying in his bunk reading when suddenly he was thrown out of it with terrific force. There was a tearing, cracking sound as if *Tzu Hang* was being ripped apart. Water burst into the cabin. Miles was buried in darkness under a great surge of water, bedding, and smashed pieces of wood. He fought his way to the surface and saw that the entire cabin top was gone, leaving a great gaping hole in the deck.

His first thought was for Beryl. Obviously she had been washed overboard by the tremendous sea that had swept the decks. He fought his way out to the cockpit and saw Beryl in the water about thirty yards away. Swimming strongly, with her head above water, she appeared unafraid and smiling. Remarkable woman that she was, her first thought was to reassure her husband. "I'm all right, I'm all right," she shouted above the howling of the wind.

The yacht had been completely dismasted. Masts and rigging were strewn in the sea on both sides of the hull. Beryl managed to reach some of this wreckage and slowly pull herself closer to the boat. Once she was alongside, John and Miles dragged her up on deck. She was bleeding from a deep cut on her forehead and she had a broken collarbone (although she didn't mention that until later).

Tzu Hang was a wreck, masts and rigging gone, hull

half full of water, a six-foot-square hole in her deck. The storm was still raging and the great seas threatened to overwhelm her at any moment. The situation looked hopeless. But these three indomitable sailors set to work at once with buckets to get the tons of water out of the hull. Slowly they began to make some progress. They were bailing for their lives and performing miracles of strength. Even Beryl with her broken bone never complained as she heaved up the heavy buckets.

With enough water out of the hull to keep *Tzu Hang* afloat, the next problem was to prevent more from getting in. John at once set to work with tools and canvas to cover the gaping hole in the deck, but even when this was accomplished, their situation still appeared hopeless. They were a thousand miles from land in the stormiest seas in the world. They had no masts, no engine, no compass, and not too much food and water. Even so, the idea of giving up—of surrendering to the sea—never crossed their minds.

Now that Miles was relieved of the backbreaking job of bailing, he had time to analyze what had happened. Running as she was before the great seas—many of them fifty feet high or higher—*Tzu Hang* had literally tripped and gone head over heels just as a running man who stumbles will fall head first, with his feet in the air. The bow of the boat had been pressed down and the stern pushed up until she had fallen over on her beam ends and rolled completely over and come up facing the other way. It was while she was upside down that her masts had been broken off by the tremendous reverse pressure of the keel.

Ever since Joshua Slocum's successful circumnavigation of the globe in the *Spray,* it has been more or less assumed by yachtsmen that a small, well-found vessel handled by skillful seamen could ride out anything the sea might offer. Examples have been offered of great ocean liners that were badly damaged while fighting their way through storms while small boats running before the wind under the same conditions bobbed up and down like ducks on the top of the waves. The cardinal rule was to go slow. If you kept the yacht from moving too fast through the water, nothing could happen to her, no matter how great the seas. It was a comforting theory, but like most such theories it was not one hundred percent true. *Tzu Hang* proved the exception. She proved that a small, able yacht, no matter how beautifully handled, can still be overwhelmed by the sea even when under bare poles and dragging ropes to slow her down.

At the moment of the crash, it was small comfort to Miles and Beryl to know they had proven something of value to all other yachtsmen. Their first job, of course, was to get the boat to land, and now that they had most of the water out of her, they began rigging a jury mast under which they might be able to carry some sort of sail, no matter how small.

John Guzzwell took over the job of building a new mast. It was a monumental job, but he tackled it with his usual skill and energy. While he was at it, Miles and Beryl

100

made some attempt to clean up the mess below. The inside of *Tzu Hang* looked as though it had been put through a gigantic mixer. The contents of every locker had been hurled out into the cabin. Broken glass, marmalade, broken eggs, and soggy bread were all mixed with soaked books, charts, and clothing. It was hardly worthwhile trying to separate anything. About all they could do was heave the mess overboard by the bucketful.

At last the new mast—only fifteen feet high but nevertheless a major accomplishment under those conditions —was up and *Tzu Hang* was sailing before the wind under a small square sail. It was then that Miles found the rudder gone—sheared right off as if by a giant cleaver. How could a yacht under jury rig travel a thousand miles without a rudder? But once again John rose to the occasion and cleverly fashioned a steering oar out of bits of scrap.

All told, they did amazingly well under their rag of sail, sometimes logging close to a hundred miles a day —until the mast broke again. But John, undaunted, set to work and built a new one. After two days of work, they had the new mast up and now, at last, the weather began to improve. The sun shone, the seas moderated, and even Beryl, who had been in great pain because of her injuries, was able to relax on deck. The mood on board was one of optimism. They made bets on when they might reach land. Beryl said a hundred days, John said fifty, and Miles said forty. Miles was almost exactly right. In the fifth week they picked up the coast of Chile and crept into port, three months after they had left Australia.

One might suppose that they would sell their wreck of a boat and swear never to go to sea again. But the Smeetons were not the kind to give up. No sooner were they ashore than they began the monumental task of rebuilding the boat. John did most of the work, doing it faster and better than any local ship's carpenter they might have found. For four months they slaved over the boat, encountering all the thousand and one delays that are inevitable on a remote coast. At the end of that time *Tzu Hang* was almost ready for sea and John, long overdue on a cruise of his own, had to leave them.

On December 9, nine months after reaching Chile, Miles and Beryl put out to sea again in *Tzu Hang*. The reasonable and safe procedure would have been to sail north along the coast to the Panama Canal and on through to the Atlantic. But Miles and Beryl had not elected to take the reasonable and safe course before and they did not elect to take it now. They were determined to round the Horn, to finish what they had started, and so they sailed south again to the region of the great storms and huge gray seas.

On Christmas Day they were in a violent storm. The barometer had dropped to 28.6 and *Tzu Hang* was reeling before the seas. The Smeetons opened their Christmas presents, petted the cat, and tried to pretend that all was well. But all was far from well. As the weather worsened and the boat trembled under the impact of the seas, they had the uneasy feeling that they had been through all this before and that once again they were headed for disaster.

At four o'clock in the afternoon, as Miles put the kettle on for tea, *Tzu Hang* heeled over, over too far, and buried herself under a raging blackness of water. As the sea burst into the ship and Miles found himself struggling for air inside the flooded cabin, all he could think was, "Oh no, not again! Not again!"

As in a nightmare, everything was repeated. The thunder of water, the cracking of wood, the heartbreaking shudder of the yacht as, upside down, she broke free of her masts. They had come to the same place, encountered the same conditions, and suffered the same incredible but identical disaster.

Tzu Hang rolled over and righted herself. Once again the Smeetons, this time without the invaluable help of John Guzzwell, began the backbreaking task of getting the water out and rigging a jury mast. Somehow they managed it and somehow, four weeks later, they were once again within sight of the coast of Chile.

It would be nice to report that the Smeetons again fixed up their boat and that *this* time they did round the Horn, but even this indomitable pair were ready at last to admit that fate or the sea gods simply would not allow them to get around Cape Horn. But they were not ready to give up their boat or the sea. *Tzu Hang* was shipped home to England to be repaired and Miles and Beryl are sailing her once more. They are unquestionably the only two people in the long history of the sea to have survived such an experience—twice.

9   *The Killer Mountain*

It is not the highest mountain in the world (Everest is 2,500 feet higher), but it is certainly the most murderous, having killed almost as many as the rest of the world's mountains put together. Its name is Nanga Parbat, and climbers everywhere feel a chill of fear at the very sound of the name.

Nanga Parbat stands alone. Its name, given to it by the Kashmir tribes, means the Naked Mountain. It stands at the far western end of the main Himalayan chain, a jagged lump of ice rising four and a half miles into the sky from the dry dusty plain. In its way it is the most awesome sight on earth. While the summit of Everest is higher, Everest rises from a base of foothills and smaller peaks all gradually forming the cone of the great mountain. Nanga Parbat has no support from any family of peaks. It stands in gloomy, frozen loneliness, the highest single mountain face on earth. To see it even from a distance is staggering. To attempt to climb it is suicidal. Assault after assault has been made on the gleaming ridges of Nanga Parbat, and each time the killer mountain has taken its toll.

The first to try was Mummery, the Englishman, one of the great climbers of the world. He was a slender, bespectacled businessman who spent his summers clambering over every bit of rock in Europe and who did as much as any man to introduce new techniques into the art of mountaineering. His great climbs in the Alps are legendary, but when he came to Nanga Parbat he met his match.

The year was 1895 and Mummery was the best-known climber in the world. Physically unimpressive—looking perhaps more like a butterfly collector than a mountaineer—he had conquered the toughest peaks of the Alps and the Caucasus and now was turning his attention to the one mountain in the world that fascinated him more than any other, Nanga Parbat in the storied Himalayas.

Mummery had not really planned to reach the summit. At that time no mountaineer had come anywhere near to scaling an 8,000-meter peak. What he wanted to do was work his way up the lower battlements in order to lay the groundwork for other assaults. He arrived with two English companions and a small group of porters and worked his way up to one of the great glaciers on the northwest slope. Thus far, all had gone well, so a few days later Mummery and two of the porters set off to go even higher. The weather was clear and the party at the base camp could see them moving easily along an ice ridge in the brilliant sunlight. They they disappeared from view and were never seen again. It is unlikely that so experienced a climber as Mummery took a misstep and fell. Probably he was caught in an avalanche and buried beneath tons of snow. The killer mountain had claimed its first victims.

For thirty-seven years after the death of Mummery, no human voice or footstep broke the loneliness of Nanga Parbat. Then, in the summer of 1932, came the second challengers, a German-American expedition. For some reason German mountaineers have always been fascinated by Nanga Parbat and have made the attempts to conquer her peculiarly their own. And the cost has been frightful.

Since Mummery had died on the northwest side, it was decided to attack the mountain from the northeast. On this side, the main face rises in a series of gigantic cliffs. Although a direct frontal assault was unthinkable, the plan was to attain the east ridge, which swept down from the summit in a great arc like the blade of a sickle. It was felt that the key to victory lay along that ridge: if it could be attained, from it the climbers could conceivably make a dash for the summit.

At first, as is the way with Nanga Parbat, all went

107

well. After three weeks of careful ascent, the party had climbed from their base camp to the east ridge. They were now at a height of 23,000 feet, with the summit only a little more than 3,000 feet away, less than a mile and a half. They established their seventh camp on the ridge and made their preparations for the final dash. At the rate at which they had been moving, another three days would see them at the top.

That was when the mountain moved—moved, that is, to stop them. It was almost as if the killer mountain had let them come this far with comparative ease only to make their eventual defeat more heartbreaking. Now Nanga Parbat seemed to gather all its great strength to repel them. Their good luck turned bad. They were suddenly plagued with illnesses of all kinds, from appendicitis to frostbite, and the good weather deserted them. A great storm blew up; for eight days, snow fell without ceasing. The camp on the ridge had to be abandoned, and then in turn the camps below.

Reeling, exhausted, frozen, the climbers fled down the mountain and away from the brute strength of Nanga Parbat. Long since abandoned was any hope of getting to the top; their only idea now was to escape with their lives. Like a shattered army they fled, leaving equipment and supplies behind. But in a way they were the luckiest of all, for none had lost his life on Nanga Parbat.

The peculiar quality of doom which pervades the mountain was to make itself felt only a few weeks later, however, when one of the leaders of the expedition fell from an Egyptian pyramid and was crushed to death on the stones below. It was almost as if the killer mountain had regretted its leniency and extracted one last toll.

There had now been two attempts and four deaths. It was only an inkling of the horror that was yet to come. Two years later, in 1934, the Germans again attacked the mountain. To understand fully their almost fanatical determination to conquer the mountain, one must know something of what was going on in Europe at the time. The Nazis were coming into power and the world was being divided into armed camps. The Nazi philosophy of the pure Nordic superman was predominant. Hitler was spurring German athletes on in his determination to impress the world with the superior quality of German courage and muscle. For the climbers on Nanga Parbat, it was conquer or die. And conquer they did not.

The expedition of 1934 was better equipped and more experienced than either of the two previous expeditions. Several of its climbers had been with the expedition of 1932 that had been driven back by the great blizzard. Even before they began the ascent, however, Nanga Parbat was showing its teeth. They had scarcely reached the base of the mountain when one of the climbers died of pneumonia. The others pushed on and reached Camp Seven on the ridge. They rested there and eventually established Camp Eight at 25,000 feet. On July 6 two of the climbers, Aschenbrenner and Schneider, moved even higher, reaching a point which they estimated to be only 800 feet from the summit. The weather was

109

German expedition on Nanga Parbat in 1934.

clear and they believed they could easily make a dash for the top the next day. They returned happily to Camp Eight, confident that Nanga Parbat would at last be defeated.

But, while they slept, the killer mountain was preparing its defenses. A great storm blew up and raged for thirty-six hours over the flimsy tents while the terrified climbers tried to hold the life-saving canvas down to the ground. Hurricane-force winds snapped the tent poles and ripped the canvas to shreds. The climbers had no choice but to retreat or die.

Aschenbrenner and Schneider, along with three of the porters, started down to Camp Four and miraculously managed to reach it despite the frightful conditions, but the rest of the party was not so lucky. The three other climbers, including their leader Merkl, and nine porters, were caught by darkness halfway between Camps Seven and Eight. They had to cling all night to the open ridge, and morning found them exhausted and frozen. One of the porters had died of exposure; the others were too weak to go on. The storm still raged. One by one the porters dropped in their tracks. That afternoon the first of the climbers died: he simply sat down in the snow and never got up again. Even their knapsacks containing food and clothing were gone, literally blown off their backs by the howling wind.

The story of their descent is a catalogue of horror. The weaker men died first, the stronger a little later. It had been five days since any of them had eaten. Merkl, the leader, and two others were crawling down on hands

111

and knees, leaving bloodstained tracks behind them. At last they too gave up and lay down in the snow, great drifts covering their bodies.

And so it ended, the most shocking disaster in the history of mountaineering. Eleven of the strongest and bravest climbers were dead and Nanga Parbat remained unconquered. The expedition that had come so close to victory had suffered the worst defeat of all.

Yet the Germans were determined to show the world that they could not be defeated by men or mountains. No sooner had the news of the disaster reached Berlin than plans were made for another expedition. It took three years to prepare it—three years of feverish activity while the killer mountain waited in icy indifference.

The 1937 expedition was one such as mountaineering had never seen before. The leader was Dr. Karl Wien, perhaps the most experienced Himalayan climber of his day. With him were the pick of Germany's mountaineers and the most sophisticated equipment yet devised. Their departure for Nanga Parbat captured the attention of the world, for Adolf Hitler was already advertising this assault on the mountain as the glorious proof of Nazi strength and endurance. In announcing victory in advance, Hitler was making it clear that his supermen would not be denied. Neither mountain nor nation could resist them. In effect, he was signing their death warrants. On the morning of June 14, seven of the German climbers and nine of their porters were at Camp Four; not one was ever seen alive again.

This time Nanga Parbat had not given the climbers even the illusion of victory. The killer mountain had struck back almost at once, sending a devastating avalanche down over the camp, wiping out not only every man but every trace of the camp. It was the most stunning blow ever suffered by a mountaineering party.

After days of searching and excavating, rescue parties at last found the tents, buried beneath ten feet of snow. The bodies were discovered still in their sleeping bags. The watches on the wrists of the dead men had all stopped at the same moment, a few minutes after twelve. Clearly, they had been overwhelmed by the avalanche as they slept.

One might have supposed that no more attempts on the killer mountain would be made, but the German climbers seemed bent on some sort of mass suicide on the slopes of Nanga Parbat. Twice more they returned to the mountain and twice more were beaten back. Their determination to conquer Nanga Parbat was no longer simply a mountaineering effort controlled by the men on the spot but a political action dictated by Adolf Hitler.

It was, in a way, the same sort of suicidal frenzy that was soon to lead the German army to destruction in the icy wastes of Russia. Just as Hitler sent the flower of German youth to their deaths in his thirst to conquer, so did he send the best of his climbers to their horrifying end on the glaciers of Nanga Parbat, the killer mountain.

10   *The Two Anns*

She was perhaps the loneliest and most frightened woman in the world. Her name was Ann Davison and she was alone on a 23-foot boat in the middle of the Atlantic.

Her story had begun in tragedy. Ann Davison was a young Englishwoman who had attempted to cross the ocean with her husband Frank in a 70-foot ketch, the *Reliance*. It had been a bad choice. *Reliance* was very old and massive, with immensely heavy sails and spars, altogether unsuited for a husband and wife to handle without a crew. But Frank and Ann went ahead with it anyway, determined to see the dream through, not only

114

putting out before they were ready, but in foul weather, too, because their creditors were less than a step behind.

For nineteen days they fought one gale after another and were swept helplessly up and down the length of the English Channel to crash at last on the rocks off Portland Bill. They managed to get off in a life raft, but Frank was drowned and Ann was fourteen hours on the raft before reaching shore.

It was a bad beginning. No one could have blamed Ann Davison if she had turned her back on the sea forever, but somehow she managed to pick up the pieces of her life and slowly the dream began to re-form. In Ann Davison was the stuff of which heroes are made: the conviction that it's better to die than to be defeated.

The sea terrified her but she would not be beaten by it. She took a job scraping and painting in a shipyard to gain experience. And very quietly, on the side, she studied navigation and sailing. All the while she was looking for a boat—a little one this time—small enough to be handled by a woman alone.

At last the proper vessel was found, by pure coincidence named the *Felicity Ann*. She was a pretty little thing—small to be sure, but well designed and very sturdy. Ann did not trust her own judgment, so she consulted a marine surveyor. His first question was, "How do you plan to use this boat?" Then, for the first time, Ann had to express in actual terms what had so far been only a secret dream. She was planning to sail alone across the Atlantic—a feat no woman in history had

115

ever accomplished, an undertaking to exhaust the strength and courage of most men.

She might have expected laughter or disbelief, but she got neither. After inspecting the boat, the surveyor looked thoughtful and said, "Well, yes, I think with some alterations *Felicity Ann* might be made suitable for that purpose."

So it was done. Her secret was out and she was committed. Now began the seemingly endless preparation for such a voyage. The rigging, sails, and engine she left to those who made a business of it, but in addition there were a thousand and one lists to be made up, for which she was responsible. Lists of provisions, lists of tools, lists of galley equipment, of engine spares, of bosun's gear, of paint, fuels, anchors, lights, ropes, wire, shackles, nuts, bolts, nails, screws, and even cup hooks. There were vitamins, bandages, antiseptics, chocolate, pepper, books, sandpaper, knives, wrenches, and a hundred other items to be gathered together—all this to be stowed away in a little 23-footer.

The work went on, and at last it became apparent that *Felicity Ann* was as ready as she would ever be. The question that remained unanswered was: how ready was Ann Davison? She knew a little navigation and a little about sailing, not as much as she ought to, but then hardly anyone ever does. But how much did she know about herself?

The question everyone asked her was: why are you doing this? It was a hard one to answer. She was doing it partly for Frank and for his unrealized dream, but it was not, after all, a thing he would have expected of her or even approved of. She was doing it mainly for herself. For publicity? For attention? Not at all. She was doing it because she was afraid to do it.

The voyage had assumed a symbolic significance for her. It seemed to her that the journey alone across the Atlantic was somehow like the journey through life. In the beginning there was the preparation and learning, then at last the great test against adversity. And if one survived and won, one could come at last into snug harbor and peacefully drop the anchor, knowing that one had taken the very worst that could ever be offered.

At last the day came when Ann Davison, ready or not, was off. The wise thing, of course, would have been to make a short preliminary voyage just to get the hang of the thing. But she thought if she did that, and somehow botched it, she might never go at all. Better to go straight away without looking back.

And so that was the way she did it. She sailed out of Plymouth, England, alone late in 1952. The sea that first day was calm, but to Ann it was terrifying. She was afraid of everything. Afraid of the wind and the sea and the ship. Afraid of reefing the sails, afraid of putting them up and of taking them down. Afraid of stopping the engine and, once having stopped it, afraid of starting it again. But most of all she was afraid of loneliness. So lonely was she in those first few hours that when a ship went by, going in a different direction, she turned to fol-

117

low it, just so she would not be entirely alone upon the sea.

Somehow she got through that first day and the first night. The sea was reasonably calm and the boat was performing well. Her fear had been replaced by a feeling of confidence. Things weren't too bad after all. Why did everyone make such a fuss about singlehanded sailing? And then—as is the way with the fates when one begins to flaunt them—fog closed in and the ship began to sink.

Before she knew it, *Felicity Ann* was half full of water, and Ann could not find out where it was coming from. She was gripped by panic. Her only thought was to find land. A more seasoned voyager would have looked first for the leak, but Ann was convinced that the vessel was sinking under her and that she must somehow reach the shore. But where was the shore? In the fog she could see nothing. All the same, she had an approximate idea of where the coast of France must be, and even in her agitation she could still steer a compass course. The wind had increased and great waves were buffeting the water-logged little craft. Ann had to go forward on the careening deck to claw down her sails. It was a risky business, and half a dozen times she was nearly washed overboard, but somehow she managed it and turned the boat for France. Fortunately, she was now in the area of French fishing boats. One of them took her in tow and brought her into Douarnenez. They bailed out the boat and anchored her securely. Poor Ann, who had not slept for four days, tumbled into her bunk.

118

Ann Davison in *Felicity Ann* as she sets sail from Plymouth, England.

Many a sailor has staggered ashore from a sinking vessel swearing he would never so much as look at the sea again. It is a vow that few keep, for one of the great strengths of the human mind is its ability to forget. And so it was with Ann.

A few days later she sailed out again, bound this time across the fearsome Bay of Biscay for the coast of Spain. And now things began to go a little better. She had a bit more knowledge of the ship and, accordingly, a little more confidence in herself. She made a good three hundred miles in five days, which, although not the speediest crossing of the Bay, is certainly not the worst. As she closed the coast, she had to put aside again all thought of sleep, because the weather was thick and there was shipping all around her. She was beginning to discover that the greatest danger to the singlehander is not the sea but exhaustion. The singlehander must sleep on a catch-as-catch-can basis and often go forty-eight hours or more without lying down.

She could hear the mournful bleat of foghorns all around her and, lacking one of her own, resorted to beating with a hammer on her frying pan. It seemed to do the trick, but the frying pan was never much good again for anything else. At length she made the port of Vigo, where she rested and refitted for the longer voyage ahead.

Her next stop was Gibraltar, five hundred miles away. Having managed to sail from England to Spain, which is

120

no mean accomplishment, Ann was enjoying a small measure of hard-won confidence. The trip to Gibraltar should not prove any more difficult. But forty hours out of Vigo she found herself in an insane world of gray skies, lashing rain, and furious winds. Little *Felicity Ann* did everything but stand on her head and, as is always the way in heavy weather, everything went wrong. The sails tore, lines got tangled, the roller reefing broke. And everything down below came adrift. The neat little world of *Felicity Ann*'s cabin was in chaos. Cups, plates, books, charts, navigation instruments, pepper, salt, and soap were hurled through the air. The galley stove came loose, to mingle with a cloud of kettles, bowls, and pans. The compass was smashed and water poured into the ship. Ann bailed desperately, until at last the storm eased.

Day after day went by. She had been without sleep for forty-eight hours and in her exhaustion began seeing things that were not there. She imagined that there were two other people on board and that one of them said, "You drop down for a nap now while I take over the watch." Obediently she did as she was told and slept until morning, when she came up to find herself alone.

Yet somehow she made it. The immense rock that is Gibraltar appeared in the distance and her weariness and discouragement were replaced by a profound sense of achievement. She had been nineteen days at sea—many of them filled with terror and hopelessness—but now all that was forgotten. She had brought *Felicity Ann* safely into port, or perhaps it was the other way around. In any case, they had made it and she could feel proud of herself and of her little ship. Ann rested, regained her strength, and prepared for the 600-mile run to the Canary Islands. This would be not only the longest leg she had attempted so far but the dress rehearsal for the real thing—the 3,000-mile voyage across the Atlantic. It would also be a major test of her navigation. It was one thing to find a port along the coast of Europe or Africa and another to locate a small island six hundred miles out in the Atlantic.

Ann Davison was twenty-nine days at sea this time, probably a record for tardiness on that particular stretch. There were several things to blame for this, and most were her own fault. Through lack of experience, she had failed to have *Felicity Ann* hauled and repainted; as a result, the ship's bottom was fouled with barnacles. The questionable water with which Ann had filled the tanks at Casablanca gave her such a severe case of dysentery that it was almost impossible for her to drag herself out of her berth. But the days of turning back were long since past. She was well out into the Atlantic now, with nowhere to go but her destination. At least the weather was not too bad. Dreamy southern days merged into calm beautiful nights. There were sunrises of crystalline clarity, and blood-red sunsets. The sharp squalls seldom lasted long, and afterward *Felicity Ann* would resume her meandering way across the lonely sea. And so at last,

122

long after her friends had given her up for dead, Ann sailed into Las Palmas in the Canaries to prepare for the final great test.

Las Palmas is the traditional jumping-off point for transatlantic voyagers. At all seasons of the year, but especially in the fall, when sailors are waiting for the hurricane season to end, small sailing craft of every description are to be found moored in Las Palmas, preparing for the final great test. Among them this time was one even smaller than *Felicity Ann:* the rubber raft of Dr. Alain Bombard, who was getting ready to cross the ocean without supplies in order to prove that a man adrift at sea could live without food or water. In addition, there was a regular League of Nations of more conventional little ships—French yachts, German and Dutch yachts, dozens of others.

For the first time, Ann found herself accepted on equal terms by this company of world voyagers. She had already proved her worth by coming this far, and no one any longer questioned her ability to make it the rest of the way.

The usual time allowance for a vessel crossing from Las Palmas to the islands of the Caribbean is about a month. The little ships sail before the trade winds and can usually sight an island of some sort within four weeks of leaving the Canaries. But Ann had been twenty-nine days from Casablanca to Las Palmas and she was no longer so optimistic about the speeds attained by her little sloop. She therefore laid in supplies not for thirty days but for sixty—and it was this foresight that saved her life.

It was the twentieth of November 1952 when Ann left the last bit of land behind her. And a bad day it was, as ragged black clouds raced before the southerly wind and rain squalls drove straight into her face. It might have been wiser to wait for better weather, but Ann had already learned the one thing that all singlehanded voyagers learn eventually. One must go on the planned date and never turn back, for if you turn back or retreat, the devils of fear that are riding so close behind may overwhelm you and in the end you may never go at all. She had already seen that many boats in Las Palmas would never leave at all and would eventually be sold by owners who had not the heart to face the great western ocean that lay ahead.

The squally weather gave way to calms and head winds, but *Felicity Ann* plugged steadily on. At the end of a week she had made a good five hundred miles, or one tenth of the journey. Fatigue and loneliness were already beginning to afflict her. One of the things that kept her going then, besides her own grit, was the knowledge that somewhere up ahead, alone on his rubber raft without so much as an apple to eat, was the brave Dr. Bombard.

The days went by. Once again Ann was afflicted by her old ailment, dysentery, and she began to feel weak and depressed. There were times when she could barely

124

drag herself out of her bunk, but the ship would not sail itself and there were always dozens of repair jobs to be done. Among other things, a lone sailor has to be electrician, plumber, mechanic, cook, navigator, and sailmaker.

Instead of the favorable trade winds she had expected, she found frustrating calms and vicious head winds. By December 6 she had made good only 667 miles and was beginning to feel desperate. Where were the long-expected trades? She was ill again and her strength was failing. How much more of this could she stand?

But then at last the wind turned fair and Ann was able to hoist her twin staysails. Under this rig, the boat would steer itself. Even while her skipper slept, *Felicity Ann* would stay on course and continue to plow westward. Ann was finally able to get a little badly needed rest and by the morning of December 8 she found to her joy that she had completed 818 miles. Although the motion of the little ship running before the quartering seas was violent, the weather was clear and she could at last begin to appreciate the beauty of the scene around her—the great foaming seas, the gorgeous golden sunrise, and the spectacular ruby sunsets.

But the good weather and fair winds were only a tantalizing promise. A week later she was plunging into vicious head seas under a black sky alive with sudden thrusts of lightning. She had now been four weeks at sea and was not yet halfway across. One hideous night of squalls

125

followed another. The ship would not steer herself at all under those conditions, and Ann was so worn out that she could barely manage to close her trembling fingers around the tiller. The rain squalls continued and the head winds made her progress painfully slow. She was seldom making good more than 35 to 40 miles a day. The situation was becoming serious. Soon she would be running short of food and water, and her strength was failing so rapidly that she did not think she would be able to handle the ship even if she did sight land. She was down to less than a pint of water a day, and in the intense heat of the southern ocean, all she could think of was her thirst.

The days went by and little *Felicity Ann* plugged to the westward, seldom making good more than one or two miles an hour. To Ann Davison it seemed that her entire life had been devoted to this endless struggle. The motion of the boat was so violent now that she could not even light her stove and had to subsist on a handful of biscuits. But she had lost her appetite anyway. The days merged into each other in a dreamlike way, so that she was hardly aware any longer of the passage of time.

At last, on January 24, the island of Dominica rose dimly on the horizon. To Ann it seemed only another hallucination, part of the nightmare of this endless voyage. Then, as she realized that it was in fact land, she roused herself from her torpor and steered the little sloop into Prince Rupert Bay.

She came up alongside one of the native schooners,

and two grinning fishermen jumped aboard to let go her anchor. She could only mumble her thanks; she would have been too weak to let it go herself.

For a long while she sat in the cockpit watching the lights of the little village spring out like fireflies in the dusk. At that moment she had no urgent desire to go ashore; it was enough to know that the land was there —that she had accomplished what she had set out to do, what no other woman had ever done before, and that to-morrow or the next day she would step ashore and talk to people and become one of them again.

II   The Long Night of the Little Boats

It was a miracle. Those who were there consider it so, and those who have studied it since are even more convinced. It was a miraculous combination of courage, effort, and good weather.

The British army lay besieged at Dunkirk in 1940, in desperate trouble. Europe had been overrun by the German armored divisions and the British had retreated into a tiny pocket on the French coast. Their backs were to the sea. They could go no farther. England and safety lay just across the Channel, but it might as well have been half a world away.

Hour by hour the German armored ring closed tighter. The troops were compressed into an ever narrowing area. At last they were on the open beach—hundreds of thousands of them waiting for the end. Overhead, the dive bombers wheeled. Behind them, the tanks and artillery roared. They turned to fight for the last time, and that was when the miracle began.

No one knows exactly how it began, how the word was spread, but somehow the message was passed that Englishmen were dying on the beaches of France and that other Englishmen must go to take them off those beaches. Small boats were needed, anything that could float and move under its own power. Lifeboats, tugs, yachts, fishing craft, lighters, barges, and pleasure boats —it was the strangest navy in history.

They poured out of the rivers and harbors and down toward the coast. Some were frowsy and hung with old automobile tires for fenders, others white and gleaming with polished chromium and flying yacht pennants. There were fishing boats, shrimp catchers, ancient car ferries that had never known the touch of salt water. Some had been built before the Boer War. There were Thames fire floats, Belgian drifters, and lifeboats from sunken ships. There were bright-blue French fishing boats and stumpy little Dutch *schouts*. There were paddle steamers and tugs pushing barges, and flatboats with ancient kerosene engines. Large and small, wide and narrow, fast and slow, they moved in a motley flood down to the shore. Some had registered with the navy and were

129

under navy command. Others had simply come by themselves, tubby little craft used for Sunday picnics on the Thames and laid up for years, somehow gotten underway by elderly gentlemen who had left their armchairs and rocking chairs. Down they came, clogging the estuaries, going off to war.

There were bankers and dentists, taxi drivers and yachtsmen, old longshoremen and very young boys, engineers, fishermen, and civil servants. There were fresh-faced young Sea Scouts and old men with white hair blowing in the wind. Some were poor, with not even a raincoat to protect them from the weather, and others were owners of great estates. A few had machine guns, some had rifles and old fowling pieces, but most had nothing but their own brave hearts.

Off they went at sundown, more than a thousand boats in all. It was a miracle that so many had been able to assemble at one place at one time, and even more miraculous that crews had been found for them. But now came the best part of the miracle. The sea, as if obedient to suggestion, lay down flat. Ordinarily the English Channel is one of the roughest places in the world—no place at all for a small boat—but suddenly the wind died and the seas subsided and the little boats went out into a calm night.

By the hundreds they poured forth. Coming up behind them, bent on missions of their own, were the warships, destroyers, cruisers, and gunboats racketing full tilt

130

across toward the coast of France. The moon was not yet up, and in the blackness—for no one dared show a light —the destroyers could not see the little boats and the little boats could not see the warships until the great gleaming bow waves moving at forty knots were right on top of them. But somehow, for the most part, they avoided each other and the strange armada moved on.

The wash thrown out by the big ships was a serious matter for the little boats, and they rocked helplessly in the wake of the warships. It was like being on a black highway with fast-moving traffic and no lights showing. A few were rammed and some were swamped, but still they moved on. Behind them, invisible in the blackness, was England. Ahead, glowing faintly from burning oil tanks and flaming artillery, lay the coast of France. On one of the little boats the man at the wheel put his arm around the shoulders of his twelve-year-old son and hugged him in silent encouragement. On another boat a girl dressed in men's clothes, having thought to fool the inspection officers by sticking an empty pipe in her mouth, now took the pipe out again and stuck it between her teeth to keep them from chattering.

Suddenly out of the night came dozens of aircraft flares dropped by the German bombers, looking like orange blossoms overhead. They lit up a nightmarish scene: wrecked and burning ships everywhere, thousands of British soldiers standing waist deep in the water holding their weapons over their heads, hundreds of thousands more in snakelike lines on the beaches. Through it all, scuttling like water bugs, moved the little boats coming to the rescue.

As the flares sputtered overhead, the planes came in to the attack. The primary targets were not the little boats but the larger ships—the destroyers and transports—but the people on the little boats fought back all the same, firing rifles and rackety old Lewis guns as the dive bombers screamed down. Exploding bombs and fiery tracers added their light to the unearthly scene. Through it all, the little boats continued to move in to the beach and began taking aboard the soldiers.

Those who were there will never forget the long lines of men wearily staggering across the beach from the dunes to the shallows, falling into the little boats, while others, caught where they stood, died among the bombs and bullets.

The amazing thing was the lack of panic. There was no mad scramble for the boats. The men moved slowly forward, neck deep in the water, with their officers guiding them. As the front ranks were dragged aboard the boats, the rear ranks moved up, first ankle deep and then knee deep and finally shoulder deep until at last it was their turn to be pulled up over the side.

The little boats listed under loads they had never been designed for. Boats that had never carried more than a dozen people at a time were now carrying sixty and seventy. Somehow they backed off the beach, remained afloat, and ferried their loads out to the larger ships wait-

A wounded soldier is hauled aboard a transport from the small craft which carried him from the shallow water near the beach.

ing offshore and then returned to the beach for more men.

As the German gunners on the coast and the German pilots overhead saw their prey escaping, they renewed their efforts. The rain of bombs, shells, and bullets grew ever greater until the little boats seemed to be moving through a sea of flame. The strip of beach, from Bergues on the left to Nieuwpoort on the right, was growing smaller under the barrage and even the gallant rear guard was now being pressed down onto the beaches. The Germans were closing in for the kill. The little boats still went about their business, moving steadily through the water.

As the situation became even more desperate, the big ships moved in right alongside the little ones, some grounding on the sand and hoping somehow to get off again despite the falling tide. Ropes, ladders, and cargo nets were heaved over the sides to make it possible for the bedraggled men to clamber aboard. Those who were wounded or too weak to climb were picked up by the little boats. Hands slippery with blood and oil clutched at other hands. Strangers embraced as they struggled to haul each other to safety. Now the fight was not only against the Germans but against time as well. The minutes and hours were racing by. Soon the gray light of dawn would be touching the eastern sky, and when it grew light the German guns and planes could pick off the survivors at their leisure. Every minute counted now; the little boats redoubled their already desperate efforts.

Orders were shouted but went unheard in that infernal din. The gun batteries shelled without stopping. To the whistle of the shells were added the scream of falling bombs and the roaring of engines, the bursting of antiaircraft shells, machine-gun fire, the explosions of burning ships, the screaming of the dive bombers.

But all this time, as if in contrast to man's frenzy, nature had remained calm. All through the spring night, the wind had not risen and the sea had remained flat. That in itself was a factor in the saving of countless lives, for if one of the usual spring gales had come whirling through the channel, rescue would have been far more difficult, if not impossible.

All through the long hours, the work went on. The old men and boys who manned the boats were sagging with exhaustion. There was an endless repetition in what they were doing: pull the men aboard, make the wounded as comfortable as possible, take them out to the larger ships, then return for more. No matter how many times they made the trip, there were still more men, apparently endless files of weary, stumbling, silent men moving down across the beaches into the water, waiting for rescue.

Sometimes the little boats ran out of gas. And sometimes the engine of a boat that had been laid up for years in a boatyard or quiet backwater simply broke down and quit. When that happened, small individual miracles were performed by grease-stained, sweating, cursing old gentlemen who whacked away in the dark with pliers and screwdrivers at the stubborn metal until some obstruction gave and the asthmatic engines ground back into life.

Meanwhile, invisible in the night sky, another battle was taking place. R.A.F. Spitfires were hurling themselves at 400 miles an hour into the massed ranks of Nazi bombers, scattering them all over the Channel. The fighters flew until they were down to their last pints of fuel and then hurriedly landed, filled their tanks and guns, and took off again. Flitting back and forth, silent as bats and deadly as hawks, they fought their own strange war at great cost to themselves and at an even greater cost to the enemy. It was thanks to them that the Germans were never able to mount a fully sustained air attack on all the motley craft beneath.

At last the ranks of men on the beach grew thinner. The flood that had once seemed endless was reduced to a trickle. Already the sky was growing light, and soon the little boats would have to scuttle away. None abandoned their position. Steadily they went on with the work. Although every minute lost might mean another life lost, the men on the beach did not panic. Slowly, steadily, silently, responding only to the orders of their officers, the long lines shuffled forward and out into the water toward the helping hands that waited for them on the little boats.

The exhausted crews looked toward the beach and saw only a handful of men left—the soldiers of the rear guard, who were still firing at the advancing Germans.

"Dawn—from the signal station, Dover—ships from the evacuation of Dunkirk coming round the south foreland and entering the gate of Dover, June 1940."—by Sir Muirhead Bone, the official Admiralty artist.

With a last quick rush, the men turned and ran for the water. In the gray light of dawn they could see the little boats bobbing there, waiting for them. The Germans, now seeing the last of their prey escaping, let loose a final barrage that turned the waterfront into a hell of flaming metal. But the little boats never budged, each waiting calmly for its load of drenched, gasping men.

And then at long last, with the fires growing pale against the daylight and the dive bombers sweeping in for the kill, the job was done, the beach was empty of life, and the overloaded fleet turned and chugged home to England.

It had been hoped that with the use of the little boats some 30,000 men might be rescued. That would have been counted an achievement of sorts. What the little boats actually did was to take off 335,000 men, the best of the British army. Although their equipment was lost, the men were not; at home in England and ready to fight again, they discouraged Hitler from any thought of invasion. Many of these same men were to land later in France along with their American allies and drive straight on through Germany to Berlin and so end the Nazi nightmare.

The fortunes of war always turn on small things, but never before has the fate of a great modern nation rested on so ill-assorted, so scruffy, so mixed a bag of strange little boats.

12   *Sunk!*

The *Trevessa* went down before dawn, quietly, like a tired old lady, with a last groan of her iron bones. She had been fighting the gale for nine days, ever since leaving Australia on May 25, 1923, bound for South Africa. An Indian Ocean gale is always fierce, and this one had been too much for the 3,000-ton *Trevessa*. She had begun to open at the seams and her pumps had been unable to handle the rising water in the hold. At last, at 1:30 on the morning of June 4, the order was given to abandon ship.

The men went quietly to the boats. There were three identical lifeboats, twenty-six feet long. Each had oars, a sail, a compass, food, water, and tobacco. The food was in the form of biscuits and condensed milk; the water—nine gallons in all—was in two beakers. The number-three boat, commanded by the first mate, Mr. Smith, carried twenty-four men. They sat straight up, shoulder to shoulder. There was hardly room to scratch.

Smith took stock of the situation. It did not appear to be so bad. The boat was terribly overcrowded and they were a very long way from land, but the radio operator had gotten off an SOS before the ship went down and there was every reason to believe that other vessels were on their way to the rescue. More than likely, they would be sighted tomorrow or the day after. In the meantime, they would hold their course in order to pick up the southeast trade winds. With their little square sail they could not hope to sail close to the wind; the best they could do was to run before it, and once they got into the trades they could run for a very long way—maybe too long. The Indian Ocean is one of the most desolate areas on the globe, and Smith knew that the nearest land was a series of tiny islands a thousand miles off. But it would not come to that, he told himself. It could not come to that.

He considered their biscuits and condensed milk and scanty supply of water. With twenty-four men, it would not last very long. They would have to be extremely careful. Best not issue any rations at all on this first day when they were still strong and well fed. He made an announcement to that effect and was surprised when it did

140

not produce the growls of protest he might have expected. The men, huddled together, drenched by spray, regarded him in glum silence. None of them expected to be in the boat very long. The matter of rations did not seem too important.

In the morning the horizon was empty. There was no rescue ship in sight, nor was there so much as a wisp of smoke in the blazing sky. Mr. Smith issued the day's rations—two tablespoons of condensed milk, one spoonful of water, and a biscuit. The same thought was in all their minds: it was not enough to live on, yet it was too much to die on. After they had eaten, each man was given a cigarette. The tobacco had no food value, but it helped a little to alleviate the thirst and general misery. The boat moved on across the oily swells, the sun merciless on their bare heads. The men were too exhausted to complain. Sitting upright, pressed together, none had been able to do anything but doze for a few minutes at a time during the night. How long could a man live with no sleep and a spoonful of water a day?

The next day it rained briefly and the men eagerly gulped the water streaming off the sail. No one realized in time that the sail had been encrusted with salt spray and the water they were drinking was brackish. It gave them violent stomach cramps and they retched helplessly.

As the sixth morning dawned, Mr. Smith looked into the faces of his crew and was frightened by what he saw. Most of the faces were covered with a reddish-brown rash which he felt indicated the onset of scurvy. Moreover, the men's legs and ankles were greatly swollen and had turned an ugly red from dangling in one position, constantly wet from the sea water in the bilge. When the daily ration was distributed, they displayed little interest. Their stomachs were so shrunken and their systems so weak that they no longer felt hunger or thirst.

No one spoke. Their throats were too dry and speaking consumed too much energy. Each man sat huddled with his own thoughts. Heat waves shimmered off the endless expanse of sea and the light was painful to the eyes. Mr. Smith tried to encourage them to keep a lookout for a passing ship, but none of the men responded.

The wind had died. The boat lay motionless under the burning sun. It was as if they had fallen off the edge of the world. Nothing moved, not so much as a fish, a bird, a cloud. The men were suffering intensely from heat and thirst. Someone came up with the idea of going over the side and hanging on to a rope to cool off in the water. Half a dozen did so, but their pleasure was short-lived. The ugly triangular fin of a shark appeared almost at once and the men clambered back aboard.

Smith stared in dismay at his crew, aware that the weakest among them could not last much longer. The following day a man named Fraser became unconscious and lapsed into a coma. They tried bathing his face and keeping a sea-soaked shirt over his head, but nothing did much good.

The next day the wind came up, the boat began to move, and Smith felt a stirring of hope. At last they were

142

on the fringe of the trade winds. Although they still had a terribly long way to go, at least they would be moving. But when he told the men that they were in the track of the trades at last, he got little response from the apathetic crew.

Fraser died and his body was given to the sea. A fragmentary burial service was muttered through parched lips as they slid the body over the side. Some felt that Fraser was the lucky one; his suffering was over.

The wind had freshened into a full gale. The lifeboat, running before it, tore along, half submerged by the giant seas. But Smith would not take in sail. They had sweltered now for two weeks in a burning furnace and he had sworn that if they ever got the wind he would drive the boat for all she was worth, no matter what. The wind would take them to land or to the bottom of the sea, but he would not stop for anything.

On they flew. Two more became unconscious. Another had gone insane. He tried to choke the man sitting next to him and at last fell gasping like a stranded fish onto the floorboards. Smith could only regard the sick men in despair. He could do nothing for them. That night, the two unconscious men died.

Now they had been eighteen days at sea and the strong wind continued. Surely, Smith told himself, they must be approaching land. As if to confirm that thought, he saw a bird, the first of the voyage. It circled over them, a bos'n bird, one of the albatross family. Although such birds have been known to range well out to sea, they usually nest on land, returning there at night. Land must be close by. But how close? Unhappily, Smith's logbook had been washed away when the heavy seas crashed over the boat in the first day of the storm, so he could no longer maintain a dead-reckoning track. That night, for the first time, he ordered the sail taken in. To run up on a reef in their weakened condition would mean death for all.

In the morning another man was dead, the fourth to go. He too was slipped over the side, while Smith mumbled the burial service. He was becoming all too familiar with it. How many more times would he have to say it? Who would say it over him when he was gone? Since their situation was now so desperate, he issued an extra ration of biscuit, but no one took it. The men's mouths were too dry to let them swallow the hard biscuit. The only thing that had kept them alive so far had been the tiny daily ration of condensed milk, but now they were even coming to the end of that. In another two days the milk would be gone.

Having lowered the sail, they knew it was now time to get it up again, but they found they had not the strength. Heaving with their skinny arms, one taking hold after another collapsed, they worked it up inch by inch. Only the strongest did the work, and their strength was no greater than that of small children. The others sat gaping in apathetic silence.

For a moment that night there was hope. Someone thought he saw a ship's light. The word was passed and

the men opened their bleary eyes to stare at the bright
white light low on the horizon. With trembling fingers
they unwrapped the flares and fired three of them. The
light remained motionless. At last they came to the despairing realization that what they had seen was only an
exceptionally bright star. One of the men, in an effort to
see better, stood up on a seat. A sudden lurch of the boat
threw him over the side. He cried out weakly. An attempt was made to steer back to him, but there was no
strength left in the helmsman's emaciated arms. The man
was gone.

The milk was finished. All they had left now was a
spoonful of water once a day for each man. They had
now been twenty-five days in the open boat, which was
riding higher in the water. Seven men were gone, and of
those that remained each had lost between thirty and
forty pounds. Smith pulled himself erect and stared up at
the sky. "God help us all. Amen," he mumbled and fell
back against the tiller.

Late that afternoon a man named Edwards called out,
"Land." No one paid attention. Delirium was common,
and anyway there had been too many false alarms. But a
few moments later Edwards repeated his cry. "Land. I
see land."

Smith peered ahead. Where for a month they had
seen empty horizon there was now a smudge. A cloud?
A mirage? He rubbed his bloodshot eyes and looked
again. It was still there and firmer now: a mountain
top sticking up above the sea like the tip of a giant

145

thumb. He remembered from his charts that only the island of Mauritius had such a prominence. He turned to the men to croak out his delight, but his voice was frozen within his dry throat. The best he could do was point with a shaking hand. Slowly the sunken faces and rheumy eyes of what had been strong young men only a few weeks before turned in the direction in which he was pointing. But they had been disappointed too many times before. They could not accept the reality of which Smith was certain but lapsed back again into their apathy and Smith had not the strength to shake them out of it.

Perhaps, he told himself, it was just as well that they did not believe in the reality of the land. It was still a long way off. A mountain top is sometimes visible fifty or a hundred miles at sea, and in a small boat that might mean another two or three days of traveling. In that time, how many more might die? They must go on, hoping for the best, knowing the reality of the mountain but still not quite believing in it. Yet, he told himself, he did believe in it. He had believed in it since that moment hours before when the croaking word, "Amen," had fallen from his lips.

In the morning the flat land at the base of the mountain was clearly visible. Smith rubbed his eyes and peered again. Yes, it was all there just as it should be according to the charts. Unquestionably Mauritius. He let the fact sink slowly through the layers of exhaustion into his benumbed brain. Mauritius. One of the most distant

146

islands of the Indian Ocean. All this time he had believed himself to be heading toward Rodriguez, but apparently the storm had blown them far off course and
they had traveled nearly a thousand miles farther. Altogether they had gone 2,300 miles, one of the longest
open-boat voyages on record. And they had survived two
violent storms and a week of burning calms—all this on
one sip of milk a day.

At sundown they were within sight of the breakers.
Smith was seized with an overwhelming desire to let the
boat go straight in to the beach, anything at all to get
ashore. But he was too much of a seaman for that.
Caught in the breakers and overturned, no man would
have the strength to swim a stroke. They must spend still
another night in the boat. Sadly he turned away, knowing that in his effort to save them all he had probably
signed the death warrant of at least one more.

That night, as they waited offshore for the dawn, Joe
Baptiste died. It seemed a double tragedy when they
were so near, but there was nothing they could do. The
only sound was the rumble of the surf and the sighing of
the wind. Ashore they could see lights and the help they
so badly needed, but it was still beyond their reach.

The dawn was a long time coming. Slowly, painfully,
the eastern sky turned from black to oyster gray. Smith
could see the reefs now and the opening between them.
With his final remaining strength he heaved over on the
steering oar and headed the boat in.

The lifeboat grounded on the sand. The men slumped

forward, tumbling over each other like so many skeletons. None had the strength to move. They waited for the people of the village, who were running down toward them now across the sand, reaching out their helping hands.

Index